Simon Tugwell

Prayer in Practice

Templegate Publishers
Springfield, Illinois

First published in 1974 by
Veritas Publications
7/8 Lower Abbey Street
Dublin 1
Ireland

© 1974 Simon Tugwell

Published in the United States of America by
Templegate Publishers
302 East Adams Street
P.O. Box 5152
Springfield, Illinois 62705
217-522-3353
templegate.com

ISBN 0-87243-099-5

Acknowledgements

The author and publishers are obliged to the following:

Irish University Press for a quotation from the CF
translation of William of St. Thierry.
Librarie Philosophique J. Vrin, Paris for permission to
translate from Festugiere, *George Herbert*.
The Division of Christian Education of the National
Council of Churches for quotations from the R.S.V.
Bible.
W.P. Watt and Son for quotations from the Grail
Psalter.

Other books by Simon Tugwell

The Beatitudes
Prayer Living with God
Ways of Imperfection
Human Immortality and the Redemption of Death
New Heaven? New Earth? Simon Tugwell (et al)

Cover: Codex Vaticanus Slavus 2, folio 163: Chronicle of
Manasses in a Bulgarian translation of the first half of the 14th
century, illustrated with a baptism of the Bulgars.

Contents

Introduction

Far and away the most important thing for us, if we want to pray, is seriously to undertake to become the kind of people who can pray, who have room for prayer, room in their lives for a God to whom they can pray. If we really do this, then prayer should, by and large, look after itself. However, it may still be useful, for our reassurance and encouragement, to fill in the picture a bit with some more specific discussion of some of the practicalities of prayer, provided that these are not taken as rubrics or techniques that can bypass the long processes of human and spiritual growth. There is no short cut to true spirituality, there is no substitute for conversion of heart.

Prayer in Practice

1 God's Gift of Prayer

We do not know what to pray
(Rom 8:26).

One very basic piece of doctrine about prayer is given us by St Paul : we do not know how to do it. "We do not know what we are rightly to pray; but the Spirit himself intercedes on our behalf with unutterable groans. And God who searches out men's hearts knows what the Spirit means, and that he is interceding for God's holy ones in accordance with God" *(Rom 8:26f)*.

It is very important for us to realise that we do not know how to pray. If we think of prayer as something that we can—or worse, that we should—master and become proficient at, we are in danger of seriously falsifying our relationship with God.

This elusiveness of prayer, this systematic impossibility of our really knowing how to do it, is an integral part of the scriptural view of prayer as something that God retains under his own control, subject to his administration.

In the Old Testament it is made very clear that man, as such, does not have the right to pray. People who presume that they have a right to approach

God, people like Nadab and Abihu *(Lev 10:1f),* pay dearly for their presumption. It is God who authorises and appoints people to pray to him. The Old Testament knows of two modes of such appointment : priestly and prophetic. Aaron and his line are appointed in the priestly way. Prophets are appointed by the direct anointing of the Holy Spirit, and they are authorised to speak to God, as it were, almost face to face and to take part in his council, by receiving from him a share in his own Spirit *(Exod 33:11; Jer 23:18).* The outstanding men of prayer in the Old Testament are all of them prophets. Moses is the great intercessor, and later Judaism also singled out Jeremiah. Of Abraham it is specifically stated, in connection with the plight of Abimelech, "He is a prophet and he will pray for you" *(Gen 20:7).*

In the New Testament the situation changes, but the doctrine remains the same. Under the new covenant all those who are in Christ are authorised to pray, because all are priests and prophets. We are all baptised into him who is prophet, priest and king; we become a priestly people, who therefore have a right to approach God, and we have all drunk of the prophetic Spirit, who inspires us to speak intimately with God as our Father.

This democratisation of prayer must not mislead us into taking it for granted. Prayer becomes a duty for us only because it is first an immense privilege. And it is a privilege that never becomes, simply, a right.

Prayer is rather like going to sleep. It is something that we certainly need, but it is not within our power to take it by storm. (Incidentally, it is worth considering whether the objection to drug mysticism may be basically similar to the objection to chronic use of sleeping pills.) Psychologically, the advice given to insomniacs is quite applicable to prayer too : instead of hounding ourselves with the thought, "I must sleep, I must pray", we are more likely to succeed if we think "I may sleep, I may pray". This attitude does not conquer sleep or prayer, but it lays us open to it.

In accordance with this conviction that prayer is not something that belongs to us by right, the early Christians were most insistent that we must not presume on any ability of our own to pray. As a priestly people we are authorised to perform acts of prayer, ranging from simple gestures like making the sign of the cross and simple recitation of the Lord's Prayer, to participation in elaborate liturgies. But the intimacy and freedom of prayer, the more prophetic element, we must be content to receive as and when it comes.

The only sense that they would be able to give to our imposing on ourselves or on each other a *rule* of prayer would be that we were going to spend a certain period of time each day engaged in liturgy, or in spiritual exercises which would dispose us for prayer, should prayer be given. To suppose that we could actually set ourselves to pray, in any intimate sense, for half an hour, they would have regarded as presumptuous if not blasphemous.

Their formula for private prayer, as we find it, for instance, in Cassian,[1] is that we must pray frequently and briefly. And "briefly" is meant as precept, not as concession. As members of the priestly community we can reasonably expect to be able to perform simple acts of prayer throughout the day— what some writers call "ejaculatory prayer". Anything more than this is a special grace, which we must receive when it comes, but should never presume on. "So prayer ought to be brief and pure, unless you are moved by the inspiration of divine grace to prolong it."[2] This is St Benedict's principle, and the continuation shows how serious their insistence was against presuming on such grace or attempting to prolong prayer in the absence of such grace : " In any case, when prayer is made in common by the community, it should always be brief".

It must not be thought that this represents just an easy way out of the difficulty of praying. If we stress the brevity of prayer, we must also stress its frequency, and this will require considerable self-discipline. Grimlac, having given St Benedict's teaching about the brevity and purity of prayer, passes immediately to consider how we can fulfil the command to pray without ceasing.[3] There should be no question of cutting prayer down to a minimum, but of finding the truest and most practical way of making our whole life prayerful.

When they tell us to pray frequently, they really

do mean frequently. At the beginning of every activity we should pray; in the course of every activity we should pray, and at the conclusion of every activity we should pray. We should of course pray when we get up in the morning and before we go to bed; we should pray at mealtimes. Eventually prayer should become so habitual that it permeates absolutely everything. Wherever we are, whatever we are doing, we should be able to refer it, in all simplicity, to the Lord, in supplication or thanksgiving or wonder or even annoyance.

Praying frequently, then, really means learning to live our whole lives with God, praying to him out of the very stuff of our lives. Often this will mean that our prayer will seem very trivial, because much that happens to us is trivial. It is in fact an excellent lesson in faith and in humility to have to pray trivial prayers. It is an exercise in faith, because it requires that we take seriously the fact that, in the Incarnation, God has penetrated all things. He has reached down even into the most trivial things of human life. Maybe St Paul was right that God does not care too much about cows *(1 Cor 9:9)*, but there is certainly nothing human that is too small for his care.

It is also an exercise in humility. Naturally we should like always to pray big prayers; but maybe we are not always big enough for big prayers. Maybe our hearts are too small to be able to contain a prayer for the peace of the world, but they can contain a very genuine prayer for the health of the pet parrot. There is a story told of a man who went out one day and prayed, "God, what is creation for?" Back came the answer : " That prayer is too big. Find a prayer your own size." Eventually he was beaten down to praying, " God, what are peanuts for?" Then he got his answer : he went back home to his laboratory and discovered some incredibly large number of different uses for peanuts.[4]

Of course our size is not something constant. Maybe it would be better to say simply that we must be content to pray the prayer that is given to us. Some days, we may find ourselves enlarged by grace and given immense responsibilities in prayer. Other days, we may find scarcely anything to say to God except, "Well, God, I'm here!"

And we must remember that we will often not actually understand the full import of what we are praying. It is the prayer of the Holy Spirit praying in us in accordance with God that really matters; that is the prayer that is heard by God. We ourselves may only hear a fraction of it. If we discern as best we can the prayer that is given us to pray, then we must be able to leave it, simply and confidently, in God's hands, not looking too anxiously to see whether or not anything comes of it. Often we should not really be able to recognise an answer to prayer if it came. Maybe the Holy Spirit was using our little prayer for some much larger purpose of his own, and his prayer may be answered even if our little prayer seems to remain unnoticed. It is in God's hands from start to finish, and we must accept that and not try to wrest it from him.

The old teaching about the brevity of prayer is really one facet of this essentially empirical approach to prayer : pray the prayer that is given, not clamouring for more, but corresponding as faithfully and accurately as possible with what is there. And this is not to go back on what we said about our freedom in our relationship with God; it means precisely that in prayer we must be free to pray the prayer that we can pray, the prayer that is right for us at the moment.

Very often all that is given is a flash of prayer, a momentary elevation of the heart to God, a sudden shout of joy or a cry for help. And if that is what is given, that is our prayer. And to build up the kind of relationship with God which makes it possible, which indeed makes it second nature to us to pray like that, we should deliberately cultivate a habit of frequent turning to God. Some people find it helpful to use quite artificial aids, like saying a little prayer every time the clock strikes. It does not matter how we do it, the important thing is that prayer should permeate our whole lives. And it is most likely to do this if we pray as often as possible out of the actual stuff of our lives.

One should certainly not despise sheer dogged effort; but the ancient tradition suggests rather strongly that such effort should be applied to building up this habit of frequent brief prayer, rather than to prolonging certain times of prayer. This way our prayer will be reasonably intense, simply because it springs out of the interest of the moment. Without in any way attaching undue importance to fervent *feelings*, it is surely still true to say, as many a medieval author said, that if we are bored by our own prayers, it is unlikely that God will be very interested in them.[5]

In fact the concern for brevity in prayer is sometimes explicitly connected with a concern for intensity. The *Cloud of Unknowing* uses the image of the man whose house is on fire. He does not make great speeches! He just flings his window open and shouts, "Fire!" Or the man who is drowning is not concerned to be eloquent, he just shouts "Help!" Our prayer should be like that.[6]

It is only if we are carried on by a certain protracted intensity that we should prolong our prayer. Giving the subjective, psychological aspect of the traditional monastic teaching, St Augustine says that we should go on praying so long as a certain "fervent intention" lasts.[7] As long as we are really involved in our praying, there is good reason to believe we should go on praying. (There is, actually, one complication that perhaps should be mentioned: St Ignatius of Loyola, in common with many others, suffered for a time the curious diabolical temptation to pray too much instead of getting a good night's sleep! He discerned in due course that it was a temptation.[8] We must never try to evaluate our prayer life outside the context of the whole of our lives. But this should not be an occasion for morbid anxiety: the devil always overreaches himself in the end, and the Lord is a good and faithful shepherd who does not desert his flock when the wolf comes.)

St Thomas, putting it very bluntly, says that when we cannot go on praying without getting bored, then it is time to stop.' There could hardly be a clearer testimony from a very great saint and theologian against the view that boredom is no obstacle to prayer!

The right place for discipline and effort and for sheer doggedness is in building up the habit of turning frequently to the Lord in the course of the day's activities and relaxations, so that we will be available for more substantial prayer if it is given, and in any case will be learning more and more how to live always in company with God.

. . . .

Is there then no room at all for setting aside specific times for prayer? Are we to give up all thought of a regular half hour or hour of mental prayer?

We must be able to treat this as a straightforwardly practical question. There is no intrinsic merit in setting aside certain periods for private prayer; it is intended as a means, and must be examined as such. If it does not lead to the desired end, it is pointless, except perhaps as an exercise in religious obedience.

Undoubtedly many people do find it helpful to set aside for themselves a certain half hour or hour every day. But it is fair to indicate that there are dangers. There is obviously the danger that we shall actually confine prayer to our appointed time and so hardly pray at all in the rest of the day, and that would be very counter-productive. There is also a more insidious danger, that we shall use our set time of prayer as a way of building up for ourselves a false sense of spiritual competence, making prayer into a spiritual property of our own, rather than a constant adventure in relationship with God. We can similarly use our regularity in prayer to give us a false sense of security. Finally, one might end up with a totally desiccated prayer life, ticking on more or less mechanically, but without reference to anything outside itself, and so sundered from its roots in the rest of our Christian life.

If we are going to give ourselves, or if we belong to a community which imposes on us, a rule for our life of prayer, I think that the best way to approach it is in terms of the old phrase *orationi vacare*. This is sometimes, very misleadingly, rendered "devote yourself to prayer". But it really means "to be available for prayer", to be free enough, on holiday enough, for prayer to be possible. This indicates the right attitude to adopt.

In the first place, we shall not be aiming to do more than place ourselves ready for prayer. We shall avoid the presumptuous supposition that we shall actually be able to pray just because we have decided to pray. The most we can do is to place ourselves ready and alert for prayer. We may do this by reading or thinking or meditating or writing or even

by just lying down and letting the turmoil in our
hearts and minds subside; we may do it by the use
of yoga postures, climbing mountains, or just sitting
half awake in church. We must discover for ourselves how best to be available for prayer, and this
must be flexible enough to allow for differing situations arising from tiredness, sickness, excitement, bad
weather, and so on.

Secondly, we must not quench the element of
"holiday". Prayer, as we have already seen, is "time
off" from playing God unto ourselves. And so it will
be counter-productive to approach our time of
prayer in a way suggestive only of business. Nor will
it be helpful to take a period of time only to sit
through it wishing it were over. I suggest that for
some people the most practical approach may be to
take usually a very short period of time, and
occasionally a very long period. A very short period
is too short for us to become unpleasantly conscious
of time; it will not make us anxious, wondering how
much longer there is. On the other hand, a very long
period gives sufficient space for us to work our way
through that kind of anxiety, and so eventually just
to surrender ourselves to a kind of temporal
spaciousness, without much sense of dimension or
direction. This is the kind of thing that happens at
an all night vigil, for instance. For some people, a
programme consisting of many very short periods, of
only a few minutes, and occasional very long periods,
may be more practical and conducive to real prayer
than a regular half hour.

The important thing is to use time in the way that fits the person concerned. There are no absolutes here. It is only the public worship of the Church that *requires* our attendance, in more or less complete indifference to our personal feelings. We must be free to explore in our private prayer, and discover the way that is right and feasible for each one individually.

Probably all of us need to make some kind of break in the day, just to stop the mad rush of business. All of us need some time for reflection, and to read the Bible and good helpful books. If in addition we decide to spend some time more specifically in readiness for prayer, we should not think that that lets us off the attempt to build up the habit of frequent prayer throughout the day. On the other hand, if we decide to concentrate on this more diffuse way of prayer, we must not for a moment think that that entitles us just to stop praying, under the impression that "to work is to pray". The true meaning of that ancient slogan is brought out very clearly by William Peraldus : our works have the force of prayer in so far as they express the image of God in us, and so appear before the throne of God just as the Son of God who is the very Image of God appears to make intercession for us. It is not our works as such, then, that can be said to constitute a kind of prayer, but our works in so far as they express the newness of life which is in us by the Spirit of Jesus, restoring the image of God in us, and so uniting us essentially with God.[10] But the Spirit who is the source of such good works is also the Spirit who prays in us, crying "Abba, Father!" to God. Our works, done in the power of the Spirit, are a kind of prayer because they spring from that basic relationship with God which the Holy Spirit establishes. But from that same source flows our conscious and explicit relationship with God, a relationship normally and naturally made explicit precisely in prayer. To claim to be in that relationship with God without ever addressing a word to him would be, at the very least, anomalous.

2 Saying our Prayers

My mouth shall show forth your praise
(Psalm 50 (51):17)

St Paul was by no means unaware of the profundities of prayer, and we have seen that he seems to regard it as systematically true that we do not know how to pray as we ought, and so have to rely on the Holy Spirit praying on our behalf in the depth of our hearts. Even so, he still seems to regard prayer as something quite simple, something that everybody can be expected to do without undue difficulty. "Do not worry about anything, but in everything let your requests be made known to God in prayer and entreaty together with thanksgiving" *(Phil 4:6)*. What kind of thing he intended, we cannot of course be sure of, but it seems very probable that he was referring to the ordinary procedure of just saying our prayers. When St Polycarp was arrested to be taken off to eventual martyrdom, he asked leave to pray for an hour. This was granted, and he just prayed, before them all, for everyone he had ever met in his life. It is taken for granted that he prayed out loud. There was nothing recondite or mystical about it, yet the old man became so engrossed in his prayer that they had to let him go on for two hours.[11]

16

In recent centuries we have come to be much more interested in the psychological, mental aspect of prayer, and as a result have, perhaps, tended to make it into something more esoteric and difficult than it need be. It is fascinating to go back once again to the middle ages and hear Peraldus explaining why prayer is such a good thing, so easy and open to everyone: "Not everyone can give alms, not everyone can fast, but everyone can pray; even if he is dumb he can pray mental prayer".[12] Mental prayer is prayer not spoken out loud, it need not be any more abstruse or mysterious than vocal prayer, only less noisy. The case is exactly parallel to that of reading. In antiquity people used to read out loud even by themselves. It was considered worthy of remark that St Ambrose read silently,[13] people used to go and watch him, it seems. But eventually silent reading came to be the norm. Similarly it was taken for granted in Christian antiquity that people would say their prayers aloud; even in the time of St Dominic people still expected to be able to hear what he was praying.[14] But gradually the practice of praying silently prevailed. But it should not be thought that this must totally change the nature of the exercise. Even if we do not always do it out loud, prayer in its simplest and most basic sense still remains a matter of saying one's prayers, having conversation with God. And there is nothing to stop us actually talking to God out loud, provided we do not unnecessarily disturb anybody else.

To see prayer in this simple way goes far to remove at least one of the major problems of prayer, that of distractions. We all know how difficult it is to keep our minds concentrated on anything for long, and if prayer has to be essentially a concentration of the mind, then of course we are in trouble. But if prayer is basically a talking to God, then we see the whole problem in a different perspective. Of course talking to God is not *exactly* the same as talking to one another, but we should not exaggerate the difference; above all, we should not think that it is only conversation with God that is mysterious! All communication is mysterious and that is one reason why our relationships with one another can often be sacramental to some extent. When we are engaged in conversation, that obviously does require a certain degree of concentration, but it is compatible also with quite a lot of distractions. When we talk to one another, there may be a hundred and one things popping in and out of our minds that are nothing whatsoever to do with our conversation, but they do not in any serious way impede communication. It is only in extreme cases that we get so distracted that conversation becomes impossible, and then surely it is time to take St Thomas' advice and stop! For practical purposes, we handle most distractions simply by not taking any notice of them, and just getting on with the conversation. It is a luxury when the house is entirely quiet and the soul completely recollected in the presence of God; and when the house is not entirely quiet, little is gained by rushing round frantically telling everyone to be silent. Even if they obey us, we shall ourselves be so het up by the end of it all that tranquillity will be out of the question. It is far better to make do with that very ordinary modicum of concentration that allows us to carry on conversations in spite of the hubbub in the background. It would be a brave man who claimed to be able to control his mind; but surely all of us can muster sufficient self-control to be able to say our prayers from time to time. And if we cannot manage to do it in absolute silence, let us not be too afraid to join the ranks of those who say their prayers out loud or at least with some movement of the lips. In fact, until very recently, it was actually in the rubrics that priests saying their Office, even by themselves, must at least move their lips.[15]

That great exponent of mental prayer, Father Augustine Baker, says in his *Inner Life of Dame Gertrude More*:[16] "It cannot be denied that for those whom vocal prayer, accompanied by some exercise of virtue (for without the latter no kind of prayer will be efficacious) is sufficient to bring to contemplation, no way is easier or more secure, none less injurious to head and health or less exposed to delusions". Coming from Father Baker, that is support indeed for those who, like St Catherine, find themselves "chattering before God".[17]

Now this obviously does not mean that we can abandon all attempt to engage our minds in our praying, and be content simply with the mere recitation of prayers. St Paul does indeed know of a kind of praying with the spirit that seems to bypass the mind, and we shall return to that later, but he also says "I will pray with my mind" *(1 Cor 14:14f)*. If there is no participation of the mind at all in our conversation with God (or with anyone else) then conversation will simply not take place in any ordinary sense. If we are too bored to listen to our own prayers, then there is no reason to suppose that God will find them any less boring.

There is actually a more general problem here about a great deal of our talking, not just in prayer. A French Dominican, Fr J. P. Manigne, published a very complicated book in 1969 called *Pour une Poétique de la Foi*, in which he suggested that modern man "has forgotten what talking means". We talk so much that we have lost the ability to distinguish between talking when we have got something to say, and just talking for the sake of talking. We have found it increasingly difficult just to sit quietly with someone, we would really prefer to have everyone talking at once. If we were less afraid of silence, we might discover once again how to say things when we have got something to say, and so discover the meaningfulness of conversation.

Philosophers have agonised for most of this century over the problem of meaning, and most of them seem to have assumed that meaning must be something quite distinct from talking, so that talking meaningfully will involve doing two different things at once: talking and then also a mystical inner act of "meaning". And surely here, as so often, philosophical nonsense reflects that of other mortals. It is widely assumed in practice, especially in connection with religious talking, that there must be some essentially mystical concomitant which makes talking meaningful: there must be something *more* to it than just talking. We have all grown cynical and suspicious from living in a world in which words are too often *mere* words.

Yet surely those other philosophers are right who say that meaningful talking is simply normal talking. The mystery, if there is one, is in unmeaningful talking; that is what needs to be explained. When I go up to someone and say "How do you do?" I will grant you that the words in themselves do not have very much obvious meaning in them; but I deny absolutely that I am putting meaning into them by some interior mystical act of Humpty Dumptyism. I am simply using a social and linguistic convention, and I may hope that I am using it correctly so that my attempt at communication succeeds. Of course, if it turned out that I was saying it to a lamp-post, there might be occasion to examine the state of my mind!

We must not become too sophisticated to be able just to talk, and this applies to our conversation with God too. The presumption is that talking does work, it is presumed innocent until proved guilty. Rather than starting with a prejudice against the sheer saying of our prayers, we should take a careful look at the various ways in which talking can, actually, misfire.

Obviously if I go up to someone with tedium and disgust written all over my face, and say "How lovely to see you!" little real communication will take place. Or if I have sat for hours looking utterly miserable, and then go up to my hostess and say profusely, "What a lovely party! I did enjoy myself!" then again my words will not mean very much. It is not that some mystical inner act of meaning is lacking, but just that my words do not fit my actual situation. No amount of inner mysticism can remedy that. Of course, there are conventions of politeness to cover some of these situations, and they may supply their own kind of meaningfulness. It would, in a different way, be odd for me to go to my hostess and say, bluntly, "I hated every minute of it".

However, if all our talking comes to be conditioned by social conventions of politeness, then once again meaningfulness will be sabotaged. We all need to have some people we trust enough not to have to be always polite with them. Your friend is, of course, someone whom you welcome with a sincere smile of genuine affection; but the sincerity of it is not just an interior sensation—after all, how is my friend to know that I am having such a sensation? The genuineness of my smile is shown in part by the fact that I do not always *have* to smile. A friend is someone you can trust enough not to have to smile at him every time you see him; if you have got a raging headache and must get your article off to the printers, and so on, maybe you will not smile at him. And this freedom not to smile, curiously, is an important part of the meaningfulness of the smile when you do smile.

It is the same with God. One can be too polite to God. If we only say the things that we consider to be expected of us, we shall never get beyond the most superficial encounter with him. Some of the saints have been notoriously blunt in their dealings with

God, and surely this is a sign of their true friendship with him.

Another way in which talking can misfire arises when we do not know how to stop talking. It is so easy for us to drift on, long after we have run out of things to say, long after we have thoroughly exhausted whatever we were talking about, just because we do not know how to stop, or are afraid to stop. Maybe we fear that we shall lose the relationship altogether as soon as talking stops. Maybe there is some dim aesthetic sense that every conversation needs a proper conclusion, instead of just petering out as conversations tend to do in practice. In the case of conversation with God, we may think that it is not respectful to God just to talk to him for two minutes and then go away. But surely that is really far more respectful and more conducive to true friendship than artificially to prolong our talking beyond the point where it signifies anything.

Of all these ways in which talking can misfire, it is obviously the first that is the most serious. Our words must fit our actual human situation. To say "Stick 'em up!" while pointing a banana at someone might be fully satisfactory in the context of a children's party, but would carry little weight in robbing a bank.

Similarly to say to God "give me humility", when I do not want humility, is self-defeating. Maybe I know that I ought to want humility; but in that case I should say, "I do not really want humility, but I know I ought to. Please make me want it." If we are too shy to say anything at all to God, then perhaps we should just sit quietly for a little while and not try to say anything. On the other hand, we may be overcome with confusion and say whatever comes into our head first. All of these are ordinary human uses of language. And we are human beings, and it is our humanity that is redeemed in Jesus Christ. So let us not be afraid to use human language in human ways when we draw close to God.

3 "Present your Bodies"

I beseech you, therefore, brethren,
to present your bodies as a living sacrifice,
holy and acceptable to God

(Rom 12:1).

St Thomas places his treatment of vocal prayer in the context of bodily prayer as a whole,[18] and learning the simplicity of just saying our prayers is only one aspect of what St Paul tells us to do when he says "Present your bodies as a living sacrifice to God". (Incidentally it is a shame that some modern translations, like the New English Bible and Today's English Version, render this "present your very selves". How anyone can maintain that ours is a materialistic age I do not know! Never have men been so ill-disposed to their own bodies as now!)

One of the great blessings we still enjoy, by and large, in our society is that we have churches; and this means that we can simply place ourselves physically in the presence of God by using the symbolism of the material building. Of course God is present everywhere, but he knows how dependent we are on bodily symbols. When our minds are empty, our hearts tired or disturbed, and our very words have run dry, then

25

we can still just dump ourselves there before the altar and present our bodies as a more or less living sacrifice to God. That should not be the absolute end of our story, but it is a beginning. St Paul certainly goes on to talk about the renewing of our minds, but that takes time, and is often not very much subject to our control.

A medieval English recluse prayed: "Ah, as thou bodily turned me from the world, turn me in heart and convert me utterly to thee with true love and belief."[19] It is as if to say, "Here I am! Come and get me".

The story is well known of the old man who used to sit for hours in church. When asked what he did, he replied, "Sometimes I sits and thinks, sometimes I just sits".

We can be far too self-conscious, far too much concerned with our interior states of mind. "Interiority" is not always a good principle. After all, we read that "the Word was made flesh", not that the Word was made mind. Of course his humanity includes a human mind and the Church fought long doctrinal battles over it. But even so the Bible says "The Word was made flesh", and there is an appropriate exteriority about our religion which we should take seriously.

In fact it is true of human psychology that very often the body is the most direct way to reach the heart. An embrace speaks more than hundreds of words, a sympathetic look or a gentle touch may do far more to soothe a troubled heart than any amount of more recondite assistance. Similarly our emotions show themselves in our bodies and can to a surprising extent actually be produced or reduced by adopting or changing one's bodily expression. The demarcation between being angry and mimicking anger is not entirely watertight.

So we should not be too coy of just presenting our bodies to God, without undue anxiety about what our hearts and minds are up to. If our minds are too distracted even for vocal prayer, we can still present our bodies in other ways.

In fact, in this hectic world of ours, maybe a very effective way of prayer is simply to stop all the frenetic bustle, by which we gratify our self-importance, and just do nothing at all. It may be a real self-sacrifice to God.

St Thomas tells us that the minimum requirement for prayer is intention, not attention.[20] If we intend to present ourselves to God, then that holds good until we change our intention, however little attention we may be able to pay to God. Such minimal prayer may not be very satisfying to us, but that may be a good thing. St Anthony the Great is supposed to have said that the best prayer of all is when you are quite unaware that you are praying,[21] and maybe that does not only apply to elevated ecstatic states of prayer. After all, we can be too self-conscious about prayer and want to be aware of our own prayer largely to satisfy our own vanity.

And of course we have, by and large, lost our nerve about the intrinsic validity of praying with our bodies. If you go up to someone and shake his hand, you would be very perplexed if he said, "What do you mean?" How on earth would one explain a handshake to someone for whom it was not self-explanatory? We regard the meaning of a handshake as something that looks after itself.

Yet when we read St Athanasius telling us, in effect, that we are created with hands to pray with,[22] we probably wonder what on earth he means. Yet it was that kind of thing that the early Christians thought of when they talked about prayer. They did not prescribe mental gymnastics; they just said that we should make the sign of the cross and say the Lord's Prayer; they related how such and such an old monk would spend the whole night standing in prayer with his hands raised and his face towards the place of sunrise. They told how St James had knees like a camel because he knelt so much.[23]

An Armenian prayer at the beginning of the liturgy contains the petition: "You stretched out your arm in creation even to the stars in the sky: strengthen our arms that our uplifted hands may intercede before you".[24]

We have often been unnecessarily shy about using our bodies to express ourselves. Yet we are told to love God not just with all our heart and mind, but also with all our *soul* (*nephesh* in Hebrew), which means that which makes a body into a living body *(Deut 6:4)*. The vitality of our bodies has its own distinct role in our total relationship with God.

So it need not only be a matter of presenting our bodies before God by just dumping them there like a sack of potatoes, as a last resort when all else fails. Bodily prayer is in itself a valuable part of prayer.

St Paul tells us to present our bodies as a *living* sacrifice, and surely this indicates that bodily movement and gesture may be involved. The early Christians were sometimes extremely energetic in their praying. St Bartholomew was reputed to genuflect a hundred times every day and a hundred times every night.[25] And that was nothing to what St Dominic achieved! St Dominic was apparently particularly devoted to genuflecting.[26] He found it soothing after a long day's working or travelling to go into church and leap up and down, genuflecting with tremendous agility, until he was drawn into more tranquil prayer; then he would stay kneeling for a while, and then resume his genuflections.

We should notice that kneeling is envisaged as a gesture as well as a posture.

Or we may prostrate ourselves before the Lord. The early monks seem to have spent a lot of their time making prostrations. Again this was seen as a gesture as well as a posture. When Johannan of Ephesus was staying in a certain Syrian monastry, he heard a tremendous noise coming from the room next to his, going on all through the night, as if there were three workmen beating hammers on the floor. It was the monk who lived there prostrating himself first throwing his hands on the floor, then his knees, and finally his head![27] St Dominic too was very keen on prostrations, though of a rather less dramatic kind.[28]

In fact St Dominic was renowned for his use of

the body in prayer. We have an early account called The Nine Ways of Prayer of St Dominic, which singles out the use of the body as the distinctive Dominican contribution to the doctrine of prayer.[29] It describes the different postures and gestures used by St Dominic. Sometimes he used to stand on tiptoe, stretching his arms right up towards heaven, like an arrow waiting to be shot up in the air; or he would stand like that with his hands open, as if to catch some blessing from on high. Or when he was reading the Bible, he would get tremendously excited and talk and gesticulate as if he were actually with the Lord, face to face.

It is not a matter of borrowing other people's gestures or of making a rubric for our prayer; but of learning to be free to express ourselves in whatever way is most appropriate to ourselves and our circumstances. It is again a matter of learning to use whatever resources we have at the moment.

When you are tired, for instance, it might very well be difficult to become recollected in quiet prayer; but there is nothing to stop you, maybe, going into your room and kissing the crucifix and then kneeling down for a little while, and then, perhaps, prostrating yourself before the Lord. And then perhaps doing it again.

St Thomas, good Dominican that he was, knew very well that it is often by the use of such bodily gestures of prayer that our hearts come to be drawn to devotion.[30] It is not necessary to do it this way, and it might be impertinent on those occasions when our hearts are already on fire and recollection is easy. But when our hearts are sluggish, it may be best to start with the body. Maybe the heart and mind will come tagging along behind.

And of course it works the other way too. If we are really drawn into prayer with fervour and devotion, then it is likely to seek expression in the body. St Dominic used to wake the brethren up at night with the "groanings and weeping" with which he prayed.[31] And in the fourth century it seems that at Jerusalem, when the Gospel was read, the whole congregation responded with "roaring and bellowing".[32] It must have been quite exciting! Cassian describes how sometimes in prayer one's joy becomes so immense and unbearable that it breaks forth in great shouts, so that "the glee of one's heart and the hugeness of its exultation penetrate into one's neighbour's cell".[33]

The Curé d'Ars is reported to have laughed when he prayed.[34] And a French Abbot commented on St Dominic that he had never seen anyone weep so much.[35]

God did not make us angels or disembodied spirits, he made us human. And so our prayer should be human. If we confine ourselves always within the limits of strict propriety, we shall be in danger of making prayer unnatural, and then no wonder we shall find it unnaturally difficult. We need not be too shy of expressing ourselves in all the ways that are natural to us. Indeed, as we learn to walk more confidently with the Lord, we may expect to grow in freedom of expression, as part of the glorious liberty of the children of God. This is obviously not a liberty for us to flaunt in self-display or to exercise in disregard of the convenience or even the conventions of others; it must be practised in simplicity and gentleness.

. . . .

Just one final remark about presenting our bodies to the Lord. There was considerable controversy in ancient monastic circles about what you should do if someone went to sleep while he was supposed to be saying his prayers. One of the reasons given for not prolonging prayer in a prostrate position was precisely the danger of going to sleep.[36] But there was another more lenient view. One highly respected Egyptian monk said, "If I see my brother going to sleep, I shall take his head and lay it gently on my lap".[37]

All is not necessarily lost if we go to sleep in prayer; in fact it may be a very real expression of faith. After all, fear of the dark is one of the devil's great weapons, and just going quietly to sleep without a care in the world is a great testimony of faith. The child, safe in his mother's arms, may well express his confidence and love by simply going to sleep. And God is our mother and invites us to precisely that kind of peace. "Truly I have set my soul in silence and peace. A weaned child on its mother's breast, even so is my soul" *(Psalm 130 (131):2, Grail).*

4 Presence to God

And Mary was sitting at the Lord's feet, listening

(Lk 10:39).

So far we have seen how we must attempt to build up a regular practice of turning frequently to God in the course of the day, in the context of a whole life lived for God and nourished by reading and meditation in the framework of the life of the Church; we have also seen that prayer need not always be a predominantly mental activity, but can be seen as a simple talking to God, or even the sheer presenting of our bodies to him. All of these things are involved in a very simple religious exercise which used to be widespread throughout Christendom and is found in all the main religions of the world: the exercise of repeating over and over again a small formula of prayer, usually one containing the name of Jesus, or corresponding divine names in other religions. The best known version of this practice at the moment is the eastern Christian "Jesus Prayer", which many people find helpful. A very similar devotion persisted in western Christendom at least until the seventeenth century,[38] but the fullest doctrine of it is to be found in the Byzantine spiritual writers, and so we shall be turning chiefly to them for inspiration in this chapter.[39]

The essential element is simply the repetition of the prayer, which makes it a very flexible practice, which can be used as an exercise in its own right, or as a simple form of prayer when one is travelling, or even as a kind of prayer that can be going on in the background of our other activities. It is a practice with deep historical roots, and may very well have originated precisely as an aid to constant remembrance of God in the midst of the business and activity of the day.

Be that as it may, for our purposes it will be easiest to treat it as an exercise in its own right, as a form of meditation. We can easily adapt it afterwards for other uses.

The simplest formula for this kind of prayer is just to repeat the name of Jesus; but in general a slightly longer formula was found preferable. The normal wording has come to be: Lord Jesus Christ, Son of God, have mercy on me. Some people like to add: have mercy on me, a sinner. But the sources are agreed that the important thing is that it should contain the holy Name. A very divergent form is found in an Ethiopic source:[40] Jesus, have mercy on me; Jesus, help me; I bless you, my living God, at all times. In English, however, the rhythmic structure of the standard form has much to recommend it: Lord Jesus Christ, Son of God, have mercy on me.

The authorities are clear that this is a form of vocal prayer, and sometimes even go so far as to insist that we must pray to Jesus in our hearts "without thoughts".

There are various reasons for this insistence, many of which do not concern us here. But there is one which is quite fundamental, and concerns the whole nature of this kind of prayer. We are to pray without thoughts because thinking about God would interfere with the simplicity and directness of our presence to him. This is not intended to be a way of making acts of the presence of God, but a way of making ourselves present to him. His presence is taken for granted, as of course it should be. I do not think about my friend when he is there beside me; I am far too busy enjoying his presence. It is when he is absent that I will start to think about him. Thinking about God all too easily leads us to treat him as if he were absent. But he is not absent.

Then again thinking about God can impede the purity of faith. Almost every time we sit down, we make a colossal act of faith in the chair we sit on. And we express our faith simply by taking it for granted and sitting down. If we do not trust the chair, then of course we shall proceed more experimentally and cautiously. In a slightly similar way, we express our faith in God by taking him for granted. Of course he is there and of course he is there with love and mercy. We do not have to conjure his presence up by making acts of thought or imagination. We *know* that he is there; and, acting upon that knowledge, we simply talk to him.

But often our talking runs dry, or worse, runs riot. And so we talk to him in utter simplicity, using a single formula of prayer, which is just sufficient to sustain a mutual presence of us to him and him to us. The spiritual writers call it prayer of the heart, because ideally it is a prayer that expresses a heart-to-heart presence of one to the other, bypassing the flurry of mental activity.

It is, then, essentially a way of presenting our bodies to the Lord in a very simple and pure act of faith.

It will help enormously if we adopt a position that is harmonious with this simple spiritual intention. We may have to explore a bit to find exactly what position suits each one individually, but some general guide-lines can be given.

The best position for most people will be sitting. If we try to kneel, for instance, we shall find that it is a position of strain and effort, which will contradict the tenor of our prayer. We are not trying to make an effort, we are not out to achieve anything; our whole stance is of very simple presence, offering ourselves to God and receiving his gift of himself.

We should not think that it is in any way disrespectful to sit for prayer. The Gospel tells us how Mary sat at the feet of Jesus, in rapt attention to him. Of later spiritual writers, the most famous "sitter" was Richard Rolle, who says in one of his poems—and this might be taken as his motto—"I sit and sing of love-longing".[41]

It is best to sit as solidly and relaxed as possible. For this it is best to choose a chair that is not too soft; and it should be high enough to enable you to sit with both feet on the ground, with the knees bent at a right angle.

It is worth experimenting to discover what posture is the most relaxed for you; it will almost certainly turn out not to be the one you first selected! Generally we sit in positions which simply cannot be maintained without considerable tension and discomfort.

We should place both feet firmly on the ground —let the floor do the work! This gives us a good foundation and lets the blood circulate freely. Then we should sit as upright as we can. This is not always easy for westerners, who on the whole do not have the habit of sitting upright. But it is in fact the most relaxed and invigorating position. One's whole torso seems to fall into place eventually around the central support of the spine. Finally one should rest both hands on one's lap, with the palm facing up, and the fist unclenched. This expresses one's openness and receptivity before God.

The head should be upright, in continuity with the spine. There is no need to make a fetish out of any of this, but it will be found from experience that the more we tend towards this upright posture, the more readily our minds and hearts will become composed.

The eyes should be shut and allowed to take a holiday. There is nothing to see. And we need not waste energy by trying to visualise things.

It may help to rock to and fro once or twice to discover one's centre of gravity; then it should be possible to maintain a basically tranquil position throughout the duration of the exercise.

Breathing should be allowed to look after itself. It will probably become deeper and slower as we relax, but we should not attempt to force or control it in any way at all.

It is a good idea then to begin by making the sign of the cross, invoking the assistance and protection of the Blessed Trinity and the power of the Cross of Christ. And then just begin, saying the prayer quietly or even without moving one's lips, provided one can sustain it with merely mental forming of the words. Many people find it helpful to say the prayer in time with their breathing, but this is not necessary. You can, for example, say half the prayer as you breathe in, and half when you breathe out.

It is important then to realise that one is not trying to do or achieve anything. One is simply there, in the presence of God. Later on there may be more energetic things to do, later on there may be a more energetic work of prayer to undertake; but for the moment, we are simply accepting, without even being self-conscious about it, accepting everything and referring everything back to our Lord in the words of the prayer.

This is prayer without thoughts. We should not try to produce beautiful thoughts about our Lord or wonderful imaginings. Nor should we try to conceptualise our presence to him and all that it might mean. The words of the prayer provide an ideal vehicle for all kinds of attitude that may occur: supplication, worship, contrition, even intercession; but we need not become self-conscious about them. Let it flow straight through to the Lord, without being packaged and labelled in our articulation.

Of course, it is unlikely that we shall actually find ourselves totally devoid of thoughts! But in this kind of prayer the thoughts simply do not matter. Ignore them, and just get on with saying the prayer. Let them chatter away, accept them in the same way that you can accept any other kind of disturbance, without anxiety, without trying to suppress it, without even latching on to the desire to suppress it or even to the thought "I am being disturbed". Just let it be.

As likely as not, without any deliberate intention on your part, you will actually find yourself chasing the first thought with a second one, such as "I must stop this—I'm not supposed to be thinking". That easily leads to an infinite regression, one thought trying to catch another. There is no need to take any notice of any of them! Thoughts are a bit like spoilt children trying to attract attention to themselves. If you ignore them, refusing to be distracted by them, then sooner or later they will get bored and go away.

All that one needs to do is just persist, firmly and quietly, in saying the prayer, letting it sustain one's spiritual concentration.

Another likely problem will be that of anxiety or annoyance. There may be somebody making a bit of a noise, for instance; or one may suddenly get scruples about whether one is praying properly, or whether one's back is straight enough, or just how much longer it is going to last. If anxiety really becomes unbearable, it is probably better to stop for a while; but otherwise one can use the prayer very precisely to carry out our Lord's injunction to cast our cares upon him. We need not even analyse or identify them: as soon as the feeling of anxiety comes, just waft it over to him by way of the prayer.

If you persevere in this kind of prayer, according to the authorities it will have an innate tendency to become deeper and more penetrating. Eventually, they tell us, it will reach the heart, the very centre of our physical and emotional being. This is the place from which all our thoughts proceed, as our Lord says *(Mt 15:19)*. The Byzantines took all this in a rather crudely anatomical sense, which need not concern us; what is important is that our prayer should reach down to the core of our being, the point of unity of our identity. This is something deeper than and underlying all our intellectual and emotional activity, so it is from here, if anywhere, that our thoughts and feelings can be "taken captive" for Christ, as St Paul says they should be *(2 Cor 10:5)*. It is when this deep centre is filled with the peace of Christ that our

thinking and feeling are "kept" in and by him
(cf. *Phil 4:7*).

According to the Byzantine theologians, if we
persevere in the use of the Jesus Prayer, in the way
they tell us, and in the context of general fidelity
to the life of faith in the Church, then sooner or later
we shall attain to what they call "prayer of the
heart". And then two closely related things will
happen. First, we shall discover ourselves. They
describe our finding of the place of the heart in terms
of a great homecoming. It is an experience full of
intense joy and peace. At last we penetrate, at least
to some extent, behind all our own masks and discover who we really are.

And that is to discover ourselves in God and
him in us. Finding the place of the heart, we shall
find it already indwelt by the Holy Spirit. So they
also call this the discovery of the Holy Spirit. And
that too is an experience of intense joy, which is
likely to overflow into fairly dramatic bodily manifestations, such as weeping or jumping up and down
in excitement.

No one can call Jesus "Lord" except by the
Holy Spirit, and so the practice of the Jesus Prayer
is implicitly prayer in the Holy Spirit. When we
penetrate its depth, it is the Holy Spirit we shall discover praying within us.

And we shall also discover that the same Spirit
is at prayer in the heart of the whole creation, as it
groans in travail (cf. *Rom 8:22*). And so this
apparently private and individualistic religious

exercise will lead us to the deepest possible awareness of our solidarity with one another and with all creation. And that too is an experience full of wonder.

I have mentioned these heights and depths of the Jesus Prayer because they indicate the full flowering to which it tends. In actual fact, of course, many people who use the Prayer will only experience a very little of this, occasional intimations or spasmodic surface indications that something important is going on below the level of consciousness. We should not embark on the Jesus Prayer as a kind of crash course in mystical experience; that would certainly be self-defeating and could be damaging.

The essence of it is utterly simple. It is a way of building up the habit of turning to the Lord, without pretensions. I have described how it can be used as a formal exercise in meditation, but if we really want to take it up, then we must let it spill over into the rest of our lives, so that it will accompany our walking about, our odd moments of leisure in the course of the day, and eventually it will come to form the background to all that we do. Since it is in itself not a mental form of prayer, it can be there even in the background of our mental work. Sometimes we may find that the prayer positively thrusts itself upon us; it may seem to take over the initiative—after all, it is in essence not our prayer at all, but the prayer of the Spirit within us.

The important thing is not that we should experience exhilaration or mystical quiet, but that we should come that little bit closer to the truth of what we are in God, so that our lives will be more open to being penetrated by grace, so that in one way or another we shall be drawn more and more to live in God's world. And there we shall find ourselves invited, in an entirely personal way, into intimacy and friendship with him.

. . . .

Note on the Rosary

There is obviously considerable similarity between the practice of the Jesus Prayer and our rosary; in fact, eastern Christians sometimes use a woollen rosary in reciting the Prayer.

Our rosary has developed along rather different lines, with increasing emphasis placed on the meditations, at the expense of the repetition of the Hail Marys. Yet it is worth noticing that one of the ancestors of the rosary is in fact precisely the practice of simply reciting a hundred and fifty Hail Marys, with no mention of any mysteries or meditations. And it is still for some people the best way to use the rosary, to treat it essentially as a kind of repetitive prayer, to pray it without thoughts, allowing one's mind to become tranquil under the influence of the repetition, so that one's spirit can concentrate very simply on the mysteries, without any discursive meditation at all. The particular mysteries will then be contemplated with affection, but not analysed or even conceptualised, except in the minute degree necessary to identify and distinguish them.

If we want to use the rosary in this way, then it must be stressed that the complete rosary consists of fifteen decades, not five. Fifteen decades allows time for the mind to become tranquil, and carries one through the whole mystery of redemption, from the Incarnation to the glory of the renewed creation in heaven. However valuable it may be to recite just five decades or even less, when one is attempting to practise mental prayer and actually think about the mysteries, perhaps using scripture readings as an aid, the use of the rosary as essentially repetitive prayer requires utter simplicity in its execution, and sufficient length of time for an effect to accumulate.

5 Feelings in Prayer

In my meditation a fire shall flame out
(Psalm 38:4, Douay)

We have noticed, en passant, abundant evidence that ancient Christians were not at all afraid of being emotional in prayer; sometimes their emotions were violent and demonstrative. In marked contrast to this, the tendency in recent centuries has been to regard feelings with considerable suspicion, and to favour rather a prayer of arid perseverance. In the past few years, however, a new reaction seems to have set in, in favour of a much more emotional piety. Can we find anything to guide and enlighten us about all this, or must we be content just to swing to and fro, to and fro, on the pendulum of fashion?

It was in the sixteenth century that some of the great controversies were fought out concerning the role of subjective experience in the Christian life, and a look at some of the issues raised then will shed some light on the matter for us.

As so often, a lot of the trouble was caused by exaggerated and unbalanced emphasis on only a part of the Christian religion. Some people were undoubtedly making exaggerated claims for subjective religion, eventually tending to reduce faith altogether to the mere feeling of being loved by God, making this more central than either the ordinary external works of the Christian life or belief in the objective truth of Christian doctrine.

Against this it was obviously necessary to take a firm stand. Typical of the reaction against it was the position adopted by the great Dominican theologian, Domingo de Soto.[42] He was by no means totally hostile to the idea of religious experience; but he drew a sharp distinction between experience and faith. For him, faith is essentially objective and is not susceptible of doubt; but experience is always systematically ambiguous. Even if you are morally certain that it is truly an experience of God, that can never amount to anything that Soto will call faith. There is always room for doubt.

This is obviously a very important point, which needed to be made. I may feel inspired without being inspired; I may feel marvellous as I kneel before the Blessed Sacrament, but that may be caused simply by a good dinner and an insensitive conscience. Conversely, I may feel awful, but "if our heart condemns us, God is greater than our heart".

Maybe we should be even more emphatic. In face of a Romantic fundamentalism of experience, which will believe "only what I can feel on my pulse", we must insist that people can be very seriously deceived about their own experience, even to the extent that they may think they are experiencing something or have experienced something that is not and never was the case.

Some years ago research was carried out into people who claimed to be quite unable to sleep. Studied carefully in ideal conditions, they were found to sleep normally right through the night, and then assert, on waking, that they had not slept a wink![43] We have already seen in chapter three*a rather more sinister example of the same thing, in the story of the American suburb driving out the black family.

We can be deceived even about our own experience of life, and this can happen to both individuals and groups. There is an even greater chance of our being deceived in the interpretation of our experience.

Nevertheless, in spite of all this, we shall end up in even worse trouble if we trust doubt more than we trust trust. We have already seen what havoc can be caused by losing our faith in gestures and in talking as being activities whose meaningfulness looks after itself. Similarly if I suspect that absolutely everything that I think I see might really just be hallucination, then I might as well poke my own eyes out. It is only within a context of basic trust in my own seeing that I can even begin to wonder, sensibly, whether perhaps that man whom I saw last night carrying his head upstairs in the coal scuttle was not really there at all.

Once doubt prevails over trust, then, like Othello, we shall find that no one can be proved innocent, even if they are innocent; it is only guilt that can be proved.

So we should not start with the conviction that feelings are always under suspicion, but with the

* This refers to chapter three of the first book in this series, *Prayer: Living with God* (Templegate, 1975).

realisation that they are not infallible. Then we can take a sensible look at the various ways in which they can misfire.

The first hazard is that they will "bounce" like bad cheques. This was a point already noted by St Aelred:[44] "The man who feels the love of God in his soul daily without laying down his own will to God's commands, does not yet love God". The feeling that we love God needs to be backed by our behaviour, our attitudes, and a certain gravitation of our interest towards God and the things of God. The feeling by itself is not a bad thing, only it is incomplete. It can become a bad thing if we accept it as a *substitute* for charity. Presumably something like that had happened in that suburb in America, a purely subjective feeling that all was well had been accepted as a substitute for genuine well-being. A glance at the actualities of the situation shows up the falseness of such a procedure.

St Bernard is quite positive about the feeling of love for God, even if it is not yet adequately backed; but it must not be rated higher than it deserves. It is a beginning, but no more.[45] So we should not despise it; it may often be the means by which our wills come eventually to be engaged. But it should be an incentive to us to go after more solid nourishment. A diet of unmitigated treacle would not be healthy.

Perhaps rather more dangerous is the feeling of unity that can arise, for instance, in an oecumenical prayer group. There is, unfortunately, good evidence that a feeling of unity can often serve as a substitute for real effort towards true unity;[46] and a consequence of that—a consequence that may well be actually desired subconsciously—is that the real differences and points at issue between people need not be faced, so that potential disharmony is quenched at the source, and much opportunity for challenging and inspiring dialogue is wasted.

Feelings can also misfire because they are artificial or contrived. The author of the *Cloud of Unknowing*, replying to a question from someone whom he clearly regards as a bit immature, warns him to scrutinise very carefully the "stirrings" he feels within himself, to see "whether they come from within by grace, or from outside in the manner of an ape".[47] It is not enough for us simply to mimic the devotion of others; our feelings must come from within, from our own heart, where God himself has given us a fountain of living waters welling up from within ourselves to eternal life. Merely because somebody else waves his arms around and shouts and sings, in complete abandon and freedom, it does not follow at all that I should be expressing my freedom by following suit. Secondhand spontaneity is no spontaneity at all. Of course emotions can be contagious; if everyone else in the room is exuberantly happy, it is quite likely to make me feel happy too. But unfortunately it is also likely to make me feel that I ought to be feeling happy, even if I am not. And that is a very different thing from true happiness.

We should never *try* to feel anything, nor should we conspire together to try to work ourselves up to a pitch of emotion. Genuine emotions appear spontaneously and unself-consciously, "like sparkle from the coal".[48] It is not for us to interfere, to produce the feelings that we consider we ought to have. We may sometimes have to use force to restrain unhelpful feelings, but even that, as we have seen, can be a dangerous procedure and is only to be used in an emergency.

Related to this is the danger of distorting our emotions. Feeling is a very subtle and delicate thing, which can only be categorised very approximately within the limits of our concepts and terminology. There are all kinds of fine gradations and blends, so to speak. Unfortunately we are prone to be impatient of all delicacy and fineness of perception, and prefer to see things in cruder and bolder colours. Rather than find enchantment in the particularities of this single, unique daisy, we dismiss it easily as "only a daisy". Similarly with our emotions; often we are not content with the emotion that is actually there, we try to push it forward, magnify it, to make it more specific and identifiable. It is easier to say, even to oneself, "Of course I love her", than to be silently and painfully aware of all the many, many different feelings involved in the relationship as it actually is. A slight, hesitant, shy emotion that might be fear or might be hope, or might even be joy . . . who can tolerate such a vague thing? So we haul it out and force it to give a name to itself; and we ruin it in the process.

We have grown deaf and impatient of the language of the heart. And so even where there is a true emotion, we easily falsify it, through sheer crudity of perception.

And finally, feelings can misfire through simply not being there at all. Like the would-be insomniacs, we may believe that we have experienced something when in fact we have not. This presumably always goes back to some kind of wish-fulfilment fantasy—one of the would-be insomniacs under observation actually sat up in the night and announced triumphantly (still fast asleep!) "I'm still awake". And so this kind of self-deception will be closely related to contrived and artificial emotions. It may be an easier option for some people to persuade themselves afterwards that they have felt such and such an emotion, than actually to work themselves up to feel it there and then on the spot.

One thing emerges very clearly from all this: that feelings, taken by themselves, are hopelessly ambiguous. They cannot prove anything and should not be taken to prove anything. One may feel brave and stand firm, one may feel brave and run away; there is no way of telling which, just from looking at the feeling.

On the other hand, feelings viewed in the whole context in which they arise may very well be significant. There is, after all, more connexion between feeling brave and being brave, than there is between feeling brave and not being brave. From my whole experience of myself, including not just my feelings but my actual performance, I should be able to

gauge fairly accurately how to assess the significance
of my feeling of braveness.

It is surely in this sense that the medieval writers
like Guigo II the Carthusian and St Bernard[49] tell
us to watch for the coming of grace, the coming of
the Lord. "Fire burns before him," St Bernard
quotes from the Psalm, applying it to our hearts
burning within us when the Lord is going to visit us
with his grace. It is not just the feeling taken by
itself that indicates the Lord's gracious presence, but
the feeling taken in conjunction with the whole effect
of God's grace in our lives.

William of St Thierry gives a long account, which
is worth quoting in full:[50] "In the affection of the
lover, the truth of her prayer becomes in her conscience, while she prays, the firm proof of the most
immediate presence of him who said: 'I am the
truth'. The Bride says therefore: 'Return, my
Beloved!' When you are gone, all is trouble. When
you turn away your face, holy affections collapse in
failure; bitterness and unreasonable sadness spring
up in the conscience. In life with the brethren,
scandals are everywhere; in solitude, the mind is in
tumult; inner light vanishes; darkness envelops and
crushes the soul. Faith languishes, hope flickers,
charity grows weary; the soul, become drunken, loses
control of itself; the body weighs down the spirit,
and the spirit the body. Prayer falters, reading is
at a standstill, meditation is dry; hardness of heart
culminates in utter sterility of spirit, and the whole
world takes up arms against this foolish wretch.

"But when you return, when you turn your face to me again, at the gladness of your countenance, at the sweetness of perceiving you, all is serenity and tranquillity. Holy happiness springs up in the conscience; the understanding is lively, zeal is fervent, love is enlightened, the spirit grows merry in God. The world seems worthless; the body is a servant; the powers increase, the virtues gain vigour. Faith is enlightened, hope is strengthened, and charity is set in order; joy in the Holy Spirit is ever present. Life with the brethren is sweet, and solitude with God still sweeter; the soul is stable and rich in the spiritual senses. Prayer is swift, reading profitable, meditation the fruit of reason, and spiritual effort brings all to a happy issue. Activity takes on seriousness, and leisure is sanctified; scandal and contradiction are met with no longer. Success calls forth humility; misfortune, fortitude. As long as you, armed in your strength, keep your court, all things you possess are in peace."

This shows how seriously the medievals took feelings in prayer; but it also shows how feelings must be "backed" by other evidence. It is a most serious error to despise consolations and experience of the sweetness of the Lord as if they were something childish—and in any case it is a serious error to despise children; it is adolescents, not mature men, who do not know how to play.

And, other things being equal, we must be able to treat consolations not just as a subjective phenomenon, but as indicative of a real presence of the Lord. Of course we know that he is present always

and everywhere; but he also woos us to a more
intimate relationship with him by making his presence
felt, or not felt, in any number of different ways. It
is this unpredictable, dynamic, vital element that
makes the relationship so intensely personal and real
to us in a way that we can appreciate and respond
to. We must, as it were, let him play hide and seek
with us, coming to us all unexpectedly, putting his
hand through the window and tickling us, then
running off, so that when we open the door to let
him in, he is gone. Then off we have to go in pur-
suit, and find him, as likely as not, leaping upon the
hills like a gazelle (cf. *Cant 5:3*ff; *2:8f*).

But this subjective relationship with God must not
become isolated from the wholeness of our Christian
life. We should never, for instance, set up experience
of God against doctrine. St Anselm prayed : "Make
me taste in love what I taste by knowledge; may I
perceive in my affections what I perceive in my
mind".[51] It is the God who has revealed himself to us
in Jesus Christ, who is made known to us by the word
of preaching and doctrine, whose presence we seek
to savour in love and devotion.

And times of consolation, as described by William
of St Thierry, should be seen not just as something
to wallow in complacently, but as affording an
opportunity for us to work and grow. As has been
said earlier, we must constantly seek to be aware both
of our actual situation, and of the resources we have
to hand. In times of spiritual dryness, our resources
are few; in times of consolation, they are abundant,

if only we will use them, to build up habits of prayer and fidelity to the ways of God. When the Christian life comes easily to us, that is no time to put our feet up!

But we must not try to stockpile good feelings. It is of the nature of feelings that they come and go, and usually not when you want them to. We must not try to perpetuate feelings, however elevated they may seem to be. We must not try to recapture them when they have gone. We must accept them when they are there and, if they are helpful and good, then, other things being equal, we should accept them with joy and gratefulness; if they are negative and unhelpful, we must find the best way to get through them with a minimum of damage. But either way, we must be a fish, and not get swamped by them.

The normal check on our feelings, as we have seen, is simply to see how they fit in with the rest of our situation, and so long as we do not suppress too much evidence, including evidence supplied by the comments of our friends, teachers, enemies, and others, we should not be too anxious about the risk of deception.

But there is also another, more internal, way of discernment, which we may hope to learn progressively as we pass through life.

In the last chapter we considered what the Byzantine spiritual writers call the discovery of the place of the heart. Traditionally, especially in western Christendom, knowledge of oneself has been seen as an indispensable part of and preparation for knowledge of God.[52] I take it that what is really envisaged is essentially the discovery of that depth within us from which our emotions, thoughts and decisions proceed. It does not require detailed psychological study of ourselves, but that we should know how to recognise our own truth, our own authenticity, and, by virtue of the same knowledge, that we should be able also to recognise our own falsehood, our own attempts at self-deception. If we can get down below the level of our own emotions and ideas, then at last we can actually look at our own emotions and ideas and see what is going on there.

Of course, this more introspective kind of discernment can never be infallible, and must never be divorced from the ordinary external processes of discernment. But surely C. S. Lewis was right when he said: "The best safeguard against bad literature is a full experience of good; just as a real and affectionate acquaintance with honest people gives a better protection against rogues than a habitual distrust of everyone".[53] The same principle applies to our own emotions: some experience of true, honest emotions, welling up from our own deepest heart, is the best protection against false emotions, superficially induced or distorted. Once we have acquired some taste for truth, we have a basis for learning to know our own hearts and becoming sensitive to our own feelings.

Going with this is what the eastern Christian writers call getting the "feeling" of God.[54] As we saw in connexion with the Jesus Prayer, there may come a time when we suddenly discover the praying of the Holy Spirit in us. This may be a very strong emotional experience, but even so there are two distinct things involved: there is the recognition of the divine presence, and there is the emotional reaction to that presence. When the emotional storm has subsided, then we may hear a "still small voice" bidding us know that God is not in the storm or the earthquake, but in something much simpler and quieter (cf. *1 Kings 19:9ff*). Our feelings, our emotions, however intense, are significant as a reaction to something other than they; and that something else, in this case, is very simple: the sheer presence of God in his love.

And so we should seek, not so much dramatic feelings, as the simple "feeling" of God. It is rather like learning to recognise the footsteps of someone you know well. Or it is like learning to recognise the style of a painter. Familiarity with his ways will enable us more and more to recognise certain patterns, certain configurations, certain little details, as signs of his artistry.

If we love him at all, then to recognise him will carry with it a certain excitement and joy. But in itself it is a very simple recognition of sheer factuality. It is not a sense of "I like this", but just of "there it is". This quiet sense of objectivity, of "there-it-is-ness" is a tremendous asset in the Christian life. It will enable us, underneath whatever storms of emotion may be raging, to rest tranquil in humility and peace. Then our emotional response will be rooted, it will proceed from the depths. Then indeed we can

C

afford to be emotional, intensely emotional if the mood so takes us. To be "high" without being "deep" is a risky business; but when the roots go down into the good rich soil of truth and integrity, then there need be no stopping us!

6 Liturgical Prayer

*They were persevering in the doctrine of
the apostles and in the communication of
the breaking of bread and in prayers*
                                    (Acts 2:42, Douay).

In our private prayer we may, indeed we must,
take the risk of freedom, expressing ourselves with
whatever riches of humanity and faith we may have
at the moment. But we can afford to take this risk
with much greater confidence if we also subject ourselves generously and regularly to the discipline of
the liturgy, in which we join with the whole Church
of Christ in prayer.

Of course liturgical prayer is something that we
are only just beginning to rediscover, and many of
us have still hardly even grasped theoretically what
the liturgy is supposed to be. "Every liturgical action,
as being the work of Christ the High Priest and of
his Body which is the Church, is par excellence a
sacred action, and nothing else that the Church does
can compare with it in its effectiveness. In our liturgy
on earth we already have a foretaste and share in
that liturgy which is celebrated in the holy city
Jerusalem, where Christ is, sitting at God's right

hand . . . with the whole company of the heavenly army we sing to the Lord a hymn of glory. . . The liturgy is the culmination to which all the Church's action tends, and the source from which all her power flows".[55] This is what the Second Vatican Council said about it, and it is going to take us a long time to realise it and embody it fully in our actual worship. But at least we should try not to go on saying, as used to be said, that liturgy is not prayer, but only preparation for prayer. The Vatican Council seems rather to be saying the opposite: our private prayer, like everything else that goes on in the Church, is preparation for liturgy.

The early Church appears to have had an acute awareness of the presence of the Holy Spirit in the Christian community; they did not ignore his presence in individual believers, but they were convinced that he is given to individuals in the context of the Church. It is the Church, in the first place, that is the temple of the Holy Spirit.

If it is true, as we said earlier, that prayer is essentially something that is given to us by God, something that we are empowered to do by the Holy Spirit, we can now see that it must follow that prayer is primarily something that takes place within the Church. Prayer is an activity of "the Spirit and the Bride" *(Apoc 22:17)*. It is because the Spirit prays that the Church prays; it is because the Church prays that we, as individuals, also pray.

And so prayer is not in the first place something that we do in our various nooks and crannies, and then occasionally come together to do collectively; it is in the first place something that we do together, as the Church, so that even when we are alone it is still as members of the one Body that we pray.

That is why the Vatican Council encourages us to gather together round our bishops in our cathedral churches: this gathering of all the faithful under their bishop expresses most perfectly the nature of Christian worship.[56]

Is all this just idle theory, high sounding but in the last resort ineffectual? Can liturgy really come to be the high point in our Christian lives, when so often it is, frankly, dull and uninvolving, if not actually unintelligible or repulsive?

Or—and this is a different problem—at a time of such incredible liturgical diversity and uncertainty, can one make anything at all of liturgy as such? Who is to say what liturgy consists of in practice?

In spite of all this, I still believe that it is possible and profitable to give a few basic principles of liturgical prayer, which need not remain pure theory.

A fundamental principle of liturgy is already indicated by St Paul, when he writes to the Corinthians (1 Cor 11:23ff) in connexion with the eucharist: "I passed on to you what I received from the Lord". Liturgical prayer is always essentially prayer that is received. It is not something that we simply make up; it is given.

This can be interpreted in different ways. We

have had, for instance, an extremely rubrical understanding of the givenness of the liturgy, according
to which it might be a serious sin for the priest saying Mass even to have his thumb in the wrong place.
It is a good thing that we have moved away from
that! At the other extreme, in the early Church it
seems that a great deal was left to the celebrant and
other ministers to decide, within general guidelines
laid down by tradition.

But however it may be interpreted, in one way
or another liturgy has always been something
received from the Lord through the mediation of
Church tradition, ultimately deriving from apostolic
authority.

It would therefore be a misunderstanding if we
were to over-react against the old excessively
rubrical approach by trying now to build our new
liturgies around our personal quirks and the whim
or fashion of the moment; it would be a mistake to
suppose that liturgy should be designed essentially
to give people a particular kind of experience, or
exultation or community or whatever.

Liturgy is essentially something given, and in
this it expresses a fundamental feature of all prayer.
Its sublime lack of concern for our personal moods
is a forcible reminder that when we come to God,
it is not to force our moods or our interests on to
him, but to receive his interests and to let him, in
a sense, share his moods with us.

If our primary model of prayer is that we should
be allowed to express ourselves to God, then we shall

probably remain terribly imprisoned within ourselves and our prayer will become hopelessly stuck at a very elementary stage.

It is far more central to prayer that we should let ourselves become involved in God, in his great enterprise of giving himself, and all the various interests and concerns that form part of this.

It is therefore a positive advantage that the liturgy does not just reflect our own concerns and interests, but confronts us with definite moods of its own.

We may come along feeling right down in the dumps and the liturgy will present us with praising psalms and alleluias. Or we may be as high as kites only to find ourselves obliged to recite penitential psalms. The prayers will in all probability have no relevance to the particular issues weighing on our minds at the moment, and may expect us to intercede for matters that do not interest us in the slightest.

All this is a challenge to us to become free enough and generous enough to be able, for the moment, to leave behind our moods and whims and even our most pressing concerns, and to engage ourselves in other moods, other interests. As long as we approach it wondering what we are going to get out of it, we are likely to remain discontented and bored. The question is much rather how far we are free enough from ourselves and in ourselves to be able to give ourselves, to put something into it. Then we shall find that it is in giving that we receive.

We may call this a kind of obediential praying, which expresses unmistakably the fact that true prayer must always take place in docility to the Holy Spirit. We must come to it prepared to serve, prepared to join in something that does not originate with ourselves. We are not in command here, and it is utterly irrelevant to complain that the liturgy does not lend itself to our purposes.

Maybe we have something to learn here from the old philosophical adage that happiness comes not from having what you want, but from wanting what you have.

If we give ourselves to it with a modicum of generosity, the liturgy should be one of the most effective ways in which our hearts are enlarged and moulded into conformity with the heart of Christ. Inviting us to be free from our own moods, it does not require of us a rocklike stolidity. It introduces us into an immense wealth and diversity of human experience. In the liturgy we find many different moods of prayer, many different facets of our relationship with God. We are led, we may say, into the different moods of the Holy Spirit, taking to himself the whole of that humanity with which the Son of God was united in his Incarnation.

This does not mean that we shall always, there and then, have a profound experience of what we are praying. And it certainly does not mean that we should try to work ourselves up to feel in our emotions the various liturgical acts we are engaged in. But it should over the years progressively enlarge our horizons, opening out to us new dimensions of the life of prayer, reminding us of aspects of prayer that we had forgotten or had never known at all. The liturgy, faithfully celebrated, should be a long term course in heart-expansion, making us more and more capable of the totality of love that there is in the heart of Christ.

It is not the immediate feeling that is important; that may or may not come. What matters is that we should be, slowly and quietly, moulded by this rehearsal for and anticipation of the worship of heaven. It is a schooling for paradise.

It is rather a misconception, therefore, to think that we should be making something of the liturgy. The truth is rather that the liturgy should be making something of us. It is therefore quite inappropriate for the celebrant or choirmaster to try to work up the people to an emotional state. This is not because dispassionate liturgy is intrinsically better—liturgy may turn out to be highly emotional. But emotion or lack of it is not what liturgy is about.

In our earthly liturgy we are, in a way, only eavesdropping, listening in on the liturgy of the saints. It is with the whole company of heaven that we worship, and it is their perfect worship which sustains and enfolds our prayer. Our participation should, of course, be as full as it can be; but it is of the nature of the case that it will never be perfect. We are doing something that is beyond us. By doing it, we may hope to become more capable of it, more capable of entering into the reality of what we perform. But in this life we shall never get more than a glimpse through a chink in the roof.

This is why we should not be too rigorist in our view of what participation in the liturgy involves. It is more important that it should have some over-all effect on us than that we should personally join in every hymn, and speak or listen to every word. We must be able to let it impinge in many different ways, so that our participation will sometimes be very evident and active, at other times more passive and obscure; our concentration will at times be very thorough and precise, and at other times it will be much more diffuse and vague. We must trust to the Holy Spirit, who is the life and soul of the liturgy, to involve us in it in whatever way suits him. And of course that entails that we do not interfere too much with each other's different ways of being involved.

Our participation in the prayer of the saints is symbolised in the fact that many of the prayers we say in the liturgy are in fact prayers of those whom the Church recognises as saints. And just as children pick up the language of those with whom they consort, so we may hope to learn the language of God's holy ones, the "language of heaven",[57] through keeping company with them and using their words.

This is one reason why it is sometimes useful to pray from a book even apart from the liturgy. There are some situations in which we dare not trust our own words. If we tried to talk freely, we know that we should only end up ranting, or in maudlin sentimentality, striking dramatic poses to cover the embarrassment of our own immaturity. At such times we can only say what we want to say by using the well-trodden path of someone else's prayer. This shows that we should not simply equate authenticity with using our own words: our own words may reek of falsehood, while we may be able, by courtesy of the words of someone else, to express ourselves truly and humbly.

How all this actually works out will vary enormously from person to person depending on their circumstances. Not everyone will be able to take part in the whole of the Church's liturgy, though we are now encouraged to participate in as much of it as we can. The simplest and most basic daily liturgy is just to recite the Lord's Prayer three times a day. This was the practice of all believers in the early Church, and it is in honour of this ancient custom that the new Liturgy of the Hours includes the recitation of the Lord's Prayer in the morning and evening office.[58]

This is something that everyone can do; and if we could really pray the Lord's Prayer with all sincerity, then we should be saints. If we could really become the kind of people who could honestly say "thy kingdom come," and "thy will be done", not adjusting the words to ourselves, but trying to adapt ourselves to the words, then what more direct way to perfect holiness could be devised?

The regular practice of fuller morning and night prayers, especially if we follow the traditional liturgical pattern for such prayers, can do much to shape our whole life into a life of faith. In the morning, we greet daylight as if it were the very dawning of all light, with wonder and joy; at the beginning of each day we seek to make a new beginning ourselves : knowing that the hours that lie ahead are pregnant with adventure and unknown possibilities, we commend ourselves to God's guidance and support.

Then at night, compline, the traditional night prayer, reminds us that sleep is a symbol of and preparation for death : we ask God's blessing on both our sleeping and our dying, and surrender ourselves confidently into his hands. This means letting go of the day that is past—when we die, we take nothing with us, and if we want to sleep we must also be prepared to let go. We must take that risk of faith, of letting down our defences in the helplessness of sleep. But we take that risk with joy, because our eyes have seen the salvation which God has worked in our midst.

Then, having given up everything to God in sleep, we receive ourselves and our world back from him in the morning, renewed once again in his love, which is "new every morning" *(Lam 3:23)*. So we arise "like new born babes, alleluia!",[59] having sloughed off the "old man" in sleep.

If we let the liturgy mould us, forming our days and weeks and years, not dragging it into the turmoil of our superficial emotions, but letting it, gently and firmly, draw us into its own rhythm, then we will find in it a true school of Christian living, a source of wisdom and inspiration, and more and more we shall find that it is not just an interruption of the day, but its very heart.

And the heart of that heart is, of course, the Mass, in which we bring ourselves symbolically in the bread and wine, offering ourselves in them on the altar, for the Lord to say to us "this is my Body", so that everything that is in us may be caught up into that divine reality, that human-divine reality, of the Body of Christ. This requires of us a complete surrender of self; if the Lord says "this is my Body", it is no longer open to us to say "it is my body". Once again the fundamental gesture is one of giving ourselves into the hands of God, but here it is most perfectly and completely expressed. In the Mass we present ourselves totally to him, and then receive ourselves back, transformed and consecrated, not as we were before in ourselves, but as we are in Christ, hidden and renewed. At the invitation to communion in the ancient liturgies the priest says "the holy things for the holy people":[60] the whole event is one great act of transubstantiation, making both us and the elements holy. It is not that we can claim to be holy in ourselves; but we have offered our unholiness, our sinfulness, and the Lord has accepted that offering and made it his own, uniting it with the mystery of his sacrificial death, in which death is destroyed, and with the mystery of his resurrection, that mystery of divine invincibility. The very un-holiness and sinfulness that we offer is "transub-stantiated" into the holiness and righteousness of God. And so we are after all a holy people, capable of participating in holy things. In one sense we have no part in any of this, it is a matter far too high for us; yet somehow, there we are, taken up into the middle of it : it is our sacrifice too.

Maybe we used to place an exaggerated em-phasis on the sacrificial aspect of the Mass; but we must beware of playing it down now in reaction. Man needs to sacrifice; part of the awful frustration of the whole world is the impossibility of offering to God a sacrifice that is adequate to him, or adequate to our need. It is only a perfect offering that would suffice, and where could we find a perfect offering? Even if we could offer everything that is ours, it would still be nothing at all beside the infinite love of God and we know that we cannot normally manage to of er even that much, because of our fears and our selfishness.

In his recent book on George Herbert, Father Festugière incidentally makes some remarks which are worth quoting about Catholic priestly spiri-tuality, centred on the sacrifice of the Mass—a sacri-fice offered, of course, not only by the priest but by all the participants in their different ways. "The priest is going to offer God to God. And everything is included in that, really, everything is there. He may

be or he may feel himself to be the most wretched of
men, the most abandoned, the most despised. He may
be or he may feel himself to be the most useless in-
strument. He may have got up in the morning sad,
tired, gloomy, broken in soul and body. He may have
the feeling that his whole life has been in vain, that he
has done no good at all. In spite of all that, now he is
offering God to God. And even if everything here
below is less than a speck of dust in the sight of God's
infinite majesty, still God is pleasing to God, God
cannot be indifferent to his own self . . ."[61]

It is surely no exaggeration to say that it is an
infinite relief that what we could not do, what we
could never hope to do, God himself has done. And
God is pleasing to God.

It shows a very shallow appreciation of eucharistic
piety to focus too much attention on the joys of
fellowship or even on our individual spiritual refresh-
ment in the Mass. The most wonderful thing of all is
that here God offers God to God on the altar of God,
and that is the most infinitely satisfying thing that
could ever be. Our essential satisfaction is that God is
satisfied. One who is detached from himself "in
receiving the holy eucharist wins a great grace of
union with God, because he is not concerned with
his own devotion and consolation; far more than any
devotion and consolation, he is concerned with the
glory and honour of God";[62] that is the opinion of
Thomas à Kempis.

This is the most perfect thing that it is given to us
to take part in in this world, and it contains our per-

fection because we have no perfection of our own apart from the perfection of God.

As I have said before, God has only one thing to say, and that is himself, and in uttering his own Word, which contains all his divine fullness, he is also uttering us his creatures. In the Mass we offer our nothingness, our worse than nothingness, and God takes it to himself, into the utterance of himself. The words "this is my Body" are an echo, a divine refraction through the prism of time, of the everlasting utterance of God's *I am*. And there are we in the middle of it.

This is an inexhaustible mystery, and of course it is far beyond our comprehension. But does it really make sense to desiderate a prayer life that is more exciting and immediate than that? We do not have to live on the heights the whole time, and God condescends infinitely to our pettiness and weakness so that he can meet us where we really are; but we must not be like urchins, scoffing at a splendour and beauty that we do not understand. We must recognise where the true summit of our relationship with God is, even if we have not yet learned to value it supremely. We should not try to tame or lower the summit just to make it more appealing to us. Through the discipline of obediential praying, through the privilege of praying even now in the company of the whole Church, we must learn to respond ever more humbly and gladly and deeply to what is given, learn to be excited by what is truly exciting, nourished by what is truly nourishing. Then, by the grace of God, we may begin to want that fullness of holiness which we re-hearse in the liturgy, we may at least begin to acquire a taste for the things of heaven, so that at the end we may be found fit and ready to celebrate the eternal eucharist with the Lord in the new creation.

7 Prayer of Petition

Let your requests be made known to God
(Phil 4:6).

It is hard, when we talk or think about prayer and about the marvels of our life with God, not to get carried away to dizzy heights, and we need to be brought down to earth again every now and then just to make sure that our roots are still firmly buried in the good soil of the Gospel. A good test case is provided by the subject of this chapter, prayer of petition. If our understanding of prayer leads us to despise or exclude the prayer of petition, then, however exalted and spiritual it may be, we must nevertheless regretfully observe that it has ceased to be Christian, when judged by the standard of the New Testament and the liturgy. It is indeed very remarkable how much of the New Testament teaching on prayer is concerned with petition. There can be no doubt in principle that we are meant to ask God for things, and to ask him for quite specific things. "In everything, with prayer and entreaty together with thanksgiving, let your requests be made known to God."

One basic reason for the importance of petitionary

prayer is that it is a part of our fundamental honesty before God. Prayer, as St Thomas says,[63] is the articulation of desire; and God hears our desires even before we articulate them. We cannot hide our hearts from him, and should not wish or try to do so. Bringing our desires out into the open in prayer is the acknowledgment that they are already known to God, and the confession that we are glad that it is so.

We should not be too impressed by the argument that if God has already heard our hearts, then there is no need to tell him in words what we desire. When God tested the heart of Abraham *(Gen 22:1ff)*, it was not so that he could find out something he did not know already; it was to bring the whole situation out into the open, so that both God and Abraham would know what was in the heart of Abraham, and each would know that the other knew. It was in the interests of the relationship between them, not just to satisfy his curiosity, that God subjected his friend to such a terrifying ordeal.

When we have desires in our heart, it is in the best interests of our relationship with God that we should be honest and open about them.

And this honesty will, of itself, sometimes help us to scrutinise our own desires. If there is something that we want but cannot bring ourselves to pray for, then it is at least possible that that particular desire stands under judgment and is found unworthy. After all, anything that we can legitimately want, we can legitimately pray for.[64]

Apart from this concern for basic honesty, there

is also an important matter of faith involved in petitionary prayer. Petitionary prayer reminds us that
God is not a God far off. He has come very close to
us and is intimately involved in all the concerns of
our human life. He is doing things in this world of
ours. Of course he does not interfere wantonly and at
random with the freedom and independence he has
given to us nor with the regularity of his creation; he
does not act in a way that would contradict the
gentleness and delicacy of his rule. But that does not
mean that he is little more than an absentee land-
lord. His lordship may be expressed in an idiom very
different from that of earthly lordship, but he is still
Lord. And in fact, by means of the Incarnation, God
has "filled all things" and has taken up the exercise
of his lordship more directly and intimately than
ever.

Prayer of petition is always an act of faith in this
immediacy of God's presence. And so, far from grow-
ing out of petitionary prayer as we mature spiritually,
we are more likely to grow into it, as our awareness
of God's presence and activity becomes wider and
more confident.

At the most basic level, then, prayer of petition
expresses our readiness to acknowledge that we stand
before the face of God who searches out the heart of
man; and that, on the other hand, God is very much
at large in this world of ours.

These two points are picked up by William
Peraldus.[65] He quotes from Ecclesiasticus: "Before
you pray, prepare your soul and do not be like a man

who puts God to the test" *(18:23)*. And his interpretation of this is that "you would seem to be putting
God to the test in your prayer, when you pray for
something that you do not want to be granted, and
do not expect to receive". If you pray for something
you do not want then, in the words which Peraldus
quotes from St Gregory, "for all your shouting you
are silent". And it is sheer impertinence to pray with
the implication, "I do not think you can do this,
God".

This indicates two ways in which we may expect
our petitionary prayer to mature. At first, it is likely
to consist chiefly in being honest about the various
things that we happen to want. It will be largely a
matter of saying to God, "wouldn't it be nice
if . . .?" And we should not in any way despise this
kind of praying. God is our loving Father, and he
invites us to come to him with the simple trust of little
children, who should not be shy of confessing their
desires.

But as we grow in the Lord, our desires should as
it were sort themselves out, so that certain more fundamental desires come to the fore, and these again
should come to be progressively more in harmony
with our true nature and with the will of God. In the
parable of the prodigal son, this is the stage at which
he learns what it is really to be hungry, to discover
an appetite far more central and compelling than the
superficial desires that had motivated him previously.

As our desires become more authentic and more
Godward, they will flow more easily and powerfully

into prayer, so that our petitions will take on a new seriousness and a new intensity.

By the same process we shall also discover that our needs and desires do bring us to God himself. It is a natural and inevitable consequence of original sin that we tend to turn to God only as a last resort. Our first thought is to go and get whatever we want for ourselves, and if that fails, to find some other way of procuring it, through money or influence or seduction.

This is why desperate situations can play a providential part in our growth, as has sometimes been suggested. It is not that God is a "god of the gaps", but that it is sometimes the gaps that allow us to recognise that he is the source of all our good.

Whatever means may be involved in our spiritual education—and that is God's business to arrange—we should come to recognise more and more clearly how necessary it is for us quite specifically to make our requests known to *God,* in all the various situations of our life.

We need not be afraid that this will lead to a lazy kind of irresponsibility. It is sometimes suggested that, rather than praying for the hungry, we should go and feed them, as if the two were mutually exclusive. But God is the source of all food, even if he gives it through me. I may indeed sometimes be the answer to my own prayer, and I cannot really pray with full generosity for my neighbour without being prepared to be involved in actually doing something for him : praying for him implies a real desire for him to be

helped, and it would be a somewhat crabbed
generosity that added the rider "but always on condition that *I* do not have to do anything about it".

But we must be honest: our generosity is sometimes crabbed. Sometimes it will reach as far as
genuinely wishing for good to be done, but not far
enough to say, like Isaiah, "Here am I : send me".
And even crabbed generosity is better than none at
all.

More importantly, sometimes it may genuinely
not be one of the good works that God has prepared
for me personally to walk in *(*cf. *Eph. 2:10)*. I may
be the answer to my own prayer; but then again, I
may not. To pray is to acknowledge the lordship of
God, who may not send me to do this particular work
for him. And heaven knows what harm and insult
can be done by self-appointed doers of good works!

As we grow in faith, we shall find more and more
that our aspirations and desires draw us first to God,
and only secondly to undertake measures for their
realisation. And as a result of this we shall also be
able to see how every job that is given to us includes
the responsibility of prayer. Blessed Humbert of
Romans reminds preachers that it is part of their
business to pray for those to whom they preach,[66]
and the same must be said of any position of
responsibility. If the source of any good works we may
have to do is God himself, then we cannot hope to
execute them properly unless they are built up on
prayer.

Secondly, as we grow in faith, we shall have a

progressively enlarged awareness of the extent of
God's presence and activity. Peraldus forbids us to
pray for things we do not expect to get. At first, there
is probably very little that we really believe that God
can do. As we walk with him and learn his ways, our
eyes will be opened and we shall begin to see that he
is not nearly as limited as we had thought.

This will, paradoxically, make it possible for us to
pray both much bigger and much smaller prayers.
When our hearts are still small in faith and love, we
may indeed be able to pray large prayers in the
liturgy, trusting in the faith and love of the whole
Church; we may, for instance, be able to pray with
the Church for the peace of the world, for the cessa-
tion of strife in Ireland, for justice in industry, and
enormous things like that. But left to ourselves, our
love will probably not be large enough to encompass
such hopes with any real concern and desire; and
even if there is the concern, we shall probably not
have sufficient faith to believe that there is anything
that God can do about it. But as we grow we may,
at least sometimes, find that we have got it in us to
make supplication on that scale.

But we shall also, by the same process, come to
realise just how detailed and affectionate God's care
is for even the smallest things of life. When we are
surrounded by hungry mosquitoes, we shall certainly
all be capable of a prayer of mere velleity :
"Wouldn't it be nice if they all went away or at least
stopped biting?" But would it necessarily occur to us
as perfectly practical that God might do this for us?

Does his lordship include, in our eyes, lordship over hungry mosquitoes?

As our faith grows, we shall recognise more and more realistically that God is there in literally every situation, however trivial, so we shall be able to take whatever happens to us or around us as an invitation to prayer. But at the same time, a well-rounded development of our spiritual life should also involve a shifting of our motivation, so that our interest will not be centred too much on the specific object of our petition, but on God himself. We shall become more aware that God's essential answer to every petition is himself, and that this answer may not always be expressed in precisely the way that we had hoped or wanted.

When Abraham was interceding for Sodom and Gomorrah *(Gen 18:22ff)*, we must believe that he was genuinely concerned for Sodom and Gomorrah; but even so he was more concerned with God. And so he did not abandon God because he failed to get what he wanted.

In fact, our essential motive for asking God for things should change, so that it will no longer be simply that we want things, but that we are beginning to enter into the joy that God has in giving. God likes giving, and this, in the last analysis, is the foundation for all prayer of petition.

We are not told the end of the story of the prodigal son, but it is surely likely that, as he grew to appreciate his father's love and generosity, he became more and more confident in asking for things, not

necessarily because he wanted them, but because it
made his father happy. So sometimes he might go
and ask for something utterly small, a bag of nuts or
a new hat, simply to please his father. Peraldus has
grasped a fundamental law of God's creation when
he says that "everything is for giving away".[67] This is
why sometimes the saints seem to pray for such
ridiculously small things, and even to demand and
get miracles, just to satisfy a passing whim. St Vincent
Ferrer is said to have produced a whole crop of out-
of-season figs once just to satisfy the fancy of a pregnant woman.[68] We should not be too solemn about
our relationship with God!

.   .   .   .

This leads us to the heart of what is sometimes
called "prophetic prayer". We have noticed often
enough that all prayer originates with God, and this
is particularly true of petitionary prayer at least when
it reaches its full maturity. St Catherine of Siena was
taught that when God wishes to bestow some blessing
on mankind, he stirs his servants to pray for it. "I am
ground of thy beseeching", he revealed to Julian of
Norwich.[69]

Some people have a very special mission of prayer
and intercession given them by the Holy Spirit, and
are led to spend a great deal of time in very specific
petitionary prayer. But all of us must be prepared, if
only in a very small way, to serve God in this kind of
prayer. We should not be put off by the high-
sounding word "prophetic". All Christians are
prophets, anointed with the prophetic Spirit, bap-

tised into Christ who is prophet, priest and king; it does not necessarily mean a spectacular public ministry, or an abundance of extraordinary phenomena and revelations. What it does mean is that all of us must be prepared to find ourselves sometimes stirred inwardly to offer prayer for some particular intention, without always knowing why, or even what its exact significance is. We should take such stirrings seriously and sensibly. We should not regard them as infallible, and they must be scrutinised in the usual way before we act on them, but they should not be simply disregarded or put off. If we find a prayer suggested that is manifestly contrary to Christian truth or Christian charity, then we should refuse it. If it is something quite ordinary that we feel drawn to pray, then nothing will be lost by our praying it. If it is something extraordinary, then we must examine it more closely.

In such examination two factors will be important. One is a good background of solid doctrine. The main purpose of this is to reassure us that certain kinds of prayer, which might seem outrageous, are legitimate. For instance, people often have qualms about praying for miracles; it was precisely to reassure us about that, surely, that our Lord chose the most outrageous possible kind of miracle to illustrate his teaching on faith (Mt 21:21). If we have faith, we shall even be able to move mountains by our prayers; by comparison, it is tame stuff just to pray for the occasional sick man to be healed, or for a tank full of water to be turned into petrol. Or we

may find ourselves impelled not just to pray for a
sick person, but actually to command them in the
name of the Lord to be well; and this too has scriptural warrant, because our Lord gave his Church
authority over disease *(Mt 10:1)*, and this authority
has sometimes been exercised by the saints, as when
St Catherine forbade people to die.[70] So if we find
something like this going on in our prayer, we must
not simply dismiss it as fantastic. It may be precisely
what the Lord requires of us.

The second factor is the rule given in scripture
for all prophetic activity, that it must be "according
to the measure of our faith" *(Rom 12:6)*. As has
already been said, this is not a constant in our lives:
sometimes we have more faith than at other times,
and indeed a sudden increase in faith in some particular regard may well be a normal feature of the
ministry of prayer.

But we should not presume on faith that we do
not have. It is important not to proceed by rubrics
here. The Bible is very insistent, for example, that
the healing ministry is a part of the Church's work;
but we must not assume, just because of that, that in
any case we meet we have the right to pray for healing. Quite apart from the fact that God may not intend to display his love in this way in this particular
situation, I must be faithful to pray only the prayer
that is given to me. I must find the prayer that I am
actually confident to pray here and now, regardless
of the wonderful prayers I may have prayed yester-
day or five minutes ago.

Secondly, it is advisable to make sure that the basis of our prayer really is faith. St Aelred warns of the danger of trying to work miracles just to show off,[n] and there is also the danger of trying to put God to the test, to require him to prove himself by doing whatever it may be that we have demanded. The basis of all prayer must be trust in him, and simple surrender to him, with no desire to build an empire for ourselves, or even to build an empire for him— that is his business, not ours.

We must pray the prayer that we find in our hearts, in an attitude of humility and trust, and then simply leave the whole thing in God's hands. We must never presume on any infallibility; we may have got it all wrong. It is usually only by hindsight that true prophets can be clearly distinguished from false (Deut 18:22), and we too shall often only see long afterwards that some of our prayers really were from God, while others, that we felt absolutely sure of at the time, fell wide of the mark.

And it is not only our fallibility that may come between our praying and the results that we looked for. We must appreciate that prophetic praying is a genuine dialogue with God. This comes out very clearly in the great intercession scenes of the Old Testament. The prophet, inspired and emboldened by God's own Spirit, takes part in God's council, and takes an active part, so that God is sometimes said to "change his mind" (e.g. Exod 32:14). But still, the prophet, even though he is acting under the inspiration of God's own Spirit, by no means always wins.

In the book of Amos there is a protracted discussion between God and his prophet *(7:1ff)*; the prophet turns down several of God's proposals and wins mercy for the people. But at the end God stands firm.

Even inspired praying is not, therefore, omnipotent. We must respect this mystery of God's will, which is so rich that to us it sometimes appears contradictory; medieval poets and dramatists loved to present it in terms of a great debate between mercy and justice, peace and truth. "God spoke once and I heard two things", as the psalmist says *(61:12* Vulg.*)*.

Even when we are most inspired, then, we must be prepared to leave matters finally in the hands of God. We must pray the prayer that we find within us with all the confidence and even with all the authority that we find there; but then we must let go of it, without anxiety, without any conceit, and let God be God.

8 Thanksgiving

Always giving thanks for everything
(Eph 5:20).

St Paul says that it is "together with thanksgiving" that we are to make known our petitions to God, and this is a recurrent theme with him. Over and over again he says "and be thankful", and indeed a certain centrality of thanksgiving is sufficiently indicated by the fact that the only sacrifice offered by Christians is that of the eucharist, which means "thanksgiving".

It goes without saying that we should be grateful for all the various blessings that we receive in life, the blessing of health and friends, of sunshine and bird-song, of faith and freedom to worship. Christians should be second to none in saying "thank you".

But St Paul seems to be saying more than this, in bidding us actually join thanksgiving to all our petitions. He is not just telling us to be grateful when we have received what we were asking for, but to say "thank you" at the very time of asking.

This draws us into further consideration of the nature of Christian petition. In all our diverse petitions, as we have seen, the essential gift that we are, at least implicitly, asking for is the gift of God himself; and this essential gift is already given. In Jesus Christ God has given himself utterly, he has spoken his last Word, in which all fullness is contained. (Notice, incidentally, that St Paul says both "all the fullness of the Godhead" and also, simply, "all fullness"—*Col 2:9; 1:19.*) So St Paul can say to the Corinthians : "Everything is yours . . . and you are Christ's and Christ is God's" *(1 Cor 3:21–23).* In Christ everything is already given, and so of course prayer must always be prayer with thanksgiving. We do not pray in doubt, but in assurance.

Yet this fullness which is in Christ and which is already ours "does not yet appear". We have been firmly gripped by the love of God, but our grip on him is still weak and imperfect and may, alas, still be broken utterly. And so we find ourselves in an extraordinary situation, poised between hope and actuality, between "please" and "thank you". The simultaneity of "please" and "thank you" reflects the whole ambiguity of the Christian condition. On the one hand, our Lord declared "it is accomplished" *(Jn 19:30)* as he gave up his life on the Cross. But yet we still await the consummation of the world. The kingdom of God has already come upon us *(Mt 12:28),* yet we still pray "thy kingdom come".

This is why it is important to be able to say both "please" and "thank you". Already in apostolic times there were those who maintained that the general resurrection had already taken place *(2 Tim 2:18),* and throughout Christian history we find people so assured of the victory and achievement of Christ that, effectively, they forget to say "please", they forget that we still have to ask for things, and to do so in a way which is open to God saying "no" to us. We cannot *presume* on the blessings of the age to come as if they were already fully manifest, as if we had already fully attained to them and to sufficient stature to be capable of receiving them in their fullness. Our prayer of petition is an essential sign that we are walking, as we must, by faith and not by pretended vision and achievement *(2 Cor 5:7)*.

On the other hand, we must pray with thanksgiving. This is one of the distinguishing marks separating prayer of true faith from putting the Lord to the test. We do not demand signs from God to reassure us that he is dependable, we do not require that he prove his worth to us. We pray in confidence because we know and thank him that he has already definitely overcome, he has proved his worth, in raising Christ Jesus from the dead.

Prayer with thanksgiving can thus be seen to be a very typical product of faith; it is the eye of faith that penetrates to the solidity of redemption through the shifting events and circumstances of life and so is enabled to view these events and circumstances with at least rudimentary prophetic intuition.

Old· Testament prophecy and that of the New Testament are both, at least indirectly, centred on Christ; but whereas Old Testament prophecy must thereby be essentially turned towards the future, New Testament Christian prophecy is more essentially

D

celebration of what is already there. There is still, of course, an element of futurity, there is still forward-looking Christian prophecy as we see in the Apocalypse. But there is nothing contained in the future which is not already contained within the presentness of Jesus Christ.

This is why the first manifestation of Christian prophecy is, in fact, praise, celebration of how wonderful God is. At Pentecost, as St Peter explained to the crowd *(Acts 2:17)*, the promised Spirit of prophecy was poured out by the risen, exalted Lord; but the immediate result was not prophecy at all as one would most naturally have expected it, but uproarious praise. And it is surely not without significance that it should have been praise uttered, under the power of the Holy Spirit, "in other tongues". Our praise of God in this curious in-between age is mysterious praise; his kingdom is truly present, but present "in a mystery",[72] so that very often we shall be caught up in a marvel of God's working that we do not fully understand. There is revelation, but there is also a hiddenness about it, and so our praise and thanksgiving is not quite of the same kind as that which will occur when everything is fully revealed at the end of time. We celebrate the victory of God in true joy, but we do not always understand at all clearly what that means. It requires a true prophetic intuition, and prophecy is always partial even then *(1 Cor 13:9)*. This praising in other tongues at Pentecost is a very apt expression of both the revelation and the mysteriousness of it all.

This two-way interrelationship between prophecy and thanksgiving is of great import for our Christian lives. To thank God in the way that is expected of us requires a readiness to penetrate beneath the surface of things, a readiness not to judge superficially. And conversely our prophetic witness must never be without its element of thanksgiving.

It is all too easy to call someone prophetic just because he has the courage to say unpopular things that maybe needed saying. But true Christian witness must always temper its criticisms and denunciations with sincere thanksgiving. It is most instructive to watch St Paul at work. He never minces his words, he has some extremely hard things to say to the Corinthians, for instance. Yet his first thought is not condemnation, but: "I thank my God for you always, because of the grace of God which was given to you in Christ Jesus" *(1 Cor 1:4)*. Even though he cannot call them spiritual at all, because they are utterly carnal *(1 Cor 3:1)*, he still thanks God for them always, because of the grace that God has given them.

It is not for us to connive at evil, but with the eye of faith we should penetrate to the true centre of things, and realise that in this world there is no one at all who is definitely lost. The most important thing about everyone in the world is that God has redeemed them, and that remains fundamental however far they may be from accepting God's gift and letting it transform them. In this world which was formerly the stronghold of sin and death, unlimited forgiveness has been unleashed; where death once prowled, life now marches in triumph, gathering all things into its joyful procession. The love of God is now supreme; evil has done its worst, and is defeated.

This is the ontological basis for that strange command to which St Paul returns several times and which he himself exemplifies in his letters, to thank God at all times for everyone and everything *(Eph 5:20)*. It is a hint we should do well to take up. When somebody treads on your toe, our Lord says "Pray for him", and St Paul adds "and be thankful". When you have just put your feet up at the end of a hard day and then someone knocks on the door, again thank God! When someone comes seeking advice that you know you are not in any way qualified to give, do not just become defensive, but thank God for him. When you miss your bus home, thank God.

Of course, this should not just become a rubric that we obey with trivial conformity. Our thanksgiving should proceed from true prophetic insight, and that grows in accordance with the measure of our faith. We should not rush into the ways of holiness, but grow into them as they become appropriate and feasible for us. But there is no harm in making a little start!

.   .   .   .

This brings us to a second important feature of Christian thanksgiving: its connexion with patience and perseverance. It is easy to praise God when everything is going well, when the sun is shining and our health is good. The acid test is whether we can go on praising him with sincerity when everything is going wrong, when you are out of work and far from home, with a headache, lost in the pouring rain, and no prospect of a bus for another two hours.

When our Lord wanted to indicate the distinguishing characteristic of the way of life he was teaching, he singled out generosity in face of hardship *(Mt 5:43ff)*. When people make unreasonable demands upon us, not only do we give in, but we go an extra mile with them; when they steal our jacket, we hand over the shirt too. When they hit us on one cheek, we turn the other. This was why Origen apparently referred to the virtue of patience as *"our patience"*.[73] It is the virtue which particularly belongs to us. It is not, of course, the most important virtue, but it is in some ways the most typically Christian virtue.

This does not mean that Christians have a morbid taste for suffering, nor does it mean that we should develop a kind of insensitivity which would make us indifferent to discomfort. Christian patience comes from a depth of joy which is strong enough to contain suffering. Our Lord did not want to suffer; he said, before his passion, "my soul *(psyche)* is disturbed" *(Jn 12:27)*, which is most comforting and reassuring for us when our soul, our psyche, is disturbed. True faith does not mean that we shall never be upset, even profoundly upset. What it does mean is that underneath the disturbance there is something even more profound, which is not disturbed. The letter to the Hebrews *(12:2)* tells us that it was for the joy that was set before him that our Lord endured his passion, and it was this joy that sustained him and made it possible for him to say that, in another sense, he *did* want to show his love by sacrificing himself in this way, he did long to consecrate himself for the sake of his brethren.

Our sacrifice of thanksgiving is the celebration and commemoration of the death of Jesus, and for us thanksgiving and suffering do belong together in a strangely intimate way. This is why some writers have ascribed such a definite priority to thanksgiving which is made in suffering.[74] Suffering is, we may say, the test of our thanksgiving; if it is robust enough to persevere when, humanly speaking, all is lost, then it is truly Christian thanksgiving.

Our Lord warns us that we shall be exposed to testing. In the garden of Gethsemane he himself faced the final onslaught of demonic powers; the devil who had "left him for a while" now returned with all his might. It was his hour, the hour of darkness. And the disciples, in spite of Jesus' warning that they must pray lest they succumb, were too weak to endure, and sought refuge, as we do when troubles overwhelm us, in sleep.

By our Lord's faithfulness, the power of darkness has been broken. But that does not mean that we shall not have our Gethsemane too. The Church must go through the same dark passage through which her Lord has gone before; it is through the oppression, the cramping narrowness of demonic onslaught, that she too hopes to win through to glory. She must be alert to pray, lest she succumb to the darkness.

The victory that has been won becomes our victory, in face of this attack, precisely by our faith. "This is the victory which overcomes the world: your faith" *(1 Jn 5:4)*. That radical terror by which Satan held all men bound, the fear of death *(Heb 2:15)*, has no more terrors now for those who believe. We can confront the fear of death because we know that even if we die, we shall live.

This means that we must be quite prepared to get hurt. Our Lord told us to expect that. We have no right to complain that we did not know it was going to be like that. The whole Bible is filled with warnings that we are going to get hurt.

The victory means, not that we shall never get hurt, not that we shall be able to "pray our way through" every situation to our own satisfaction and comfort; but that we can afford to get hurt, we can afford to die. Death itself is doomed, evil must eventually collapse upon its own hollowness. The whole "world" of sin is being eaten away from inside by the worm of salvation. The evil and disorder in ourselves, the evil and disorder that attack us from outside, all that is subject is fatality: it must die, and there will be an end of it. But meantime the inner man is being made new by the Spirit of God (cf. *2 Cor 4:16*).

That is the victory that bursts forth in thanksgiving. Thanksgiving is the vigour, the triumphalism, of faith. The old monks regarded psalmody as a great weapon against the devil; Alexander Akoimetes, in the best Syrian tradition, calls the psalter our "whole spiritual armour", and St Anthony once said "I psalmed down the devil".[75] And indeed one of the psalms says in so many words: "You have found praise to foil your enemy" *(Ps 8:3)*.

When St Dominic travelled through dangerous and difficult terrain, through flood and storm and the threat of murder, his response was to sing the louder, especially hymns to the Holy Spirit and to our Lady.[76]

As the darkness gathers round, we should not lose heart, but lift up the sound of praise and rejoicing. This is the hour of glory, this is the nub of St Paul's doctrine that we must rejoice *always* in the Lord.

It is my opinion that this is why exorcism, incidentally, is done in such a dramatic way. It is not strictly necessary to make a drama out of it, the simple, insistent word of command in the name of Jesus is all that is strictly necessary. It is for the sake of the exorcist and those taking part in the exorcism that we brandish crucifixes and speak with raised voices; it is to sustain our faith that we repeat with such relish in so many different ways the declaration of the power and victory of Jesus Christ. It is the atmosphere of jubilee that reinforces our own hearts against the insidious attack of devilry, whose aim is always to undermine our hope. The devil is not interested in possessing our bodies, except perhaps as an incidental amusement, and he detests the carnal sins he incites us to commit—he is, after all, a fastidious spirit.[77] What he wants is to make us despair and conclude that all is darkness, everywhere, for all time. It is against this creeping insinuation that we sing and shout "Alleluia!"

St Paul must have surprised the Colossians by saying so bluntly to them: "You are dead" *(3:3)*. And moderns are sometimes shocked by the eager way in which the old spiritual writers took up this thought. But it is, rightly understood, a most wonderful and liberating doctrine. To say that we are dead does not mean that we are afraid of or have a distaste for life; it means that we are fully alive, but that our life is, as St Paul says, not this half-and-half life here below, but an unimaginable fullness of life hidden in God and waiting to be revealed at the last day. To say that we are dead means that death has already finished with us. That is why the devil need not, in the last analysis, really scare us. However much he may hurt us, he has not got anything more that he can really do to us. His power is bluff, and his only true weapon is deceit.

By faith we live in Christ and he in us; we have been taken out of the world of darkness and transferred to his kingdom of light. Already, however dimly we perceive it, we have been made citizens of heaven *(Phil 3:20)*. And so with all our fellow citizens in glory, we too praise and celebrate God with infinite joy. Even while we wait and suffer and struggle, yearning for the final revelation of our sonship, which will bring about the total and evident renewal of all things in Christ, even while we cry out to God in prayer and entreaty, "How long, O Lord, how long?", even now it is right and fitting for us to lift up our hearts and give thanks to the Lord our God.

9 The Communion of Saints

The morning stars sang together and
all the sons of God shouted for joy
(Job 38:7)

"Since we have such a great cloud of witnesses all around us, let us too run through patience the race that lies before us" *(Heb 12:1)*. With these words the writer to the Hebrews crowns his long catalogue of the ancient heroes of faith. Our enterprise of faith, which we undertake "looking towards Jesus, the pioneer of faith", is not isolated, but takes place within a whole history of faith, stretching out down the ages, and reaching out to its culmination in that city "whose maker and builder is God", to which we draw close, even in this life, by our faith.

We are not alone, we are surrounded by all those who have tried, in their different ways and different times, to live out their divine calling in faith and that endurance which Origen calls "our patience".

God knows, because he has made it so, that human beings need each other and are mutually dependent on one another. "I might well have endowed men in body and soul with all things needful to them, but I preferred that one should have need of the other", as the Lord said to St Catherine of Siena.[78] It is therefore in no way improper that

99

our faith, whose central focus is always Jesus the
pioneer of faith and our leader, should also draw us
to our fellow men who have gone before us and are
now with the Lord.

In the first place, as the letter to the Hebrews
suggests, they can encourage us by their example. Of
course, our Lord is our prime exemplar, but he is,
if one may say so, too perfect, too complete. The
Incarnation is, as the early Church loved to reflect,
a way in which God the incomprehensible and
immense makes himself small enough for us to see.[79]
But this same courtesy of God led him also to let us
see his light not just as it is in itself, but also refracted
through the prism of creatures, broken down into a
rich diversity of colours that are easier for us to
appreciate than the unrelenting purity of light in
itself. The fundamental exemplar for all humanity
is of course Jesus Christ himself, but his perfection
is reflected for us in the created perfection of men
and women, the "just who have been made perfect"
that the letter to the Hebrews talks of later in the
same chapter.

It encourages our faith to see not only that the
offer of grace is there in Christ, not only that our
humanity is renewed in its totality in him, but that
particular men and women, men and women like us,
have received that grace, and that their particular
humanity has been renewed.

It is not weakness of faith that seeks comfort and
support in this way; this is a law of God's creation,
the law of our human interdependence.

But the mystery of our involvement with those who have gone before is more than this. The saints are not just like those tiresome people who, having taken the plunge, call to us who stand and shiver on the brink how lovely it really is in the water!

The saints are closer to us than that: in some way we already share in their victory. Their victory is not external to us, inciting us from outside to win our victory. We are one Body in Christ, members of one another; and, as St Paul teaches, if one member of the Body is sick, the whole Body suffers with it, and if one member of the Body is glorified, then the whole Body rejoices *(1 Cor 12:26)*. We share in the well-being of those who have been perfected in Christ. The perfection of the saints of the Old Testament was not to be "without us" *(Heb 11:40)*, and even the saints of the New Testament are still waiting for the full number of God's chosen ones to be gathered in *(Apoc 6:9ff)*, so that in some mysterious way they are not separated from our weakness. But yet—and once again we meet the radical ambiguity of the Christian era, in which we must wait mysteriously for what already is—the saints are declared to be "perfect", their lot is to be "with Christ" *(cf. Phil 1:23)*; and we are not separated from their perfection. We are all one Body, interconnected in one single life vivifying all the different limbs and holding them together in unity.

This is the basis for the doctrine of indulgences. The treasure which the saints have in Christ is a treasure that is shared with the whole Body of Christ.

Indeed, the fundamental law which Peraldus summed up so neatly in the phrase "everything is for giving away" applies even more to spiritual treasures than to material good things. God's gifts are for giving away, for sharing. We receive them as essentially gift, as something to be given again, not to be hoarded. There is no one so poor as the rich man who thinks to himself "this much is mine" and so excludes himself from sharing in all the rest. Everything is for giving away, just as in our physical bodies every organ receives life only in sharing it. If the life is the blood, as the Hebrews thought, it is of the essence of blood that it circulates; if it stops circulating, we begin to die.

If it is still possible to use the ruined word "charismatic", this is the charismatic dimension of the Christian life. Blessings are not given for us to hoard, but to share; sometimes they are given to us quite simply for somebody else, and hardly concern us at all—except in so far as, of course, we share in all the gifts that are given to anyone. If I have a gift of healing, the person who benefits is the person healed, not the healer. And of course this is the everyday experience of every priest, exercising the ministry given to him at his ordination. Ordination does not necessarily give him anything at all for himself; he may be an atrocious priest. But he is given all manner of good gifts to give away to other people in the sacraments.

Everything is for giving away in God's world, and those who have been delivered from the half-light of this present age and are with the Lord must surely see this far more clearly than we can. They must know, as Aristotle glimpsed,[80] that a man who has got everything still needs a friend, because his everything would not be complete unless he had someone to share it with. The saints cannot be possessive about the glory, the joy, the life that is theirs; united with him who did not clutch greedily at his own divinity but emptied himself for our sake, they too pour out the bliss that is theirs into the Body from which they are not separated, so that what they have, we too may have.

Our Christian life is not lived in splendid isolation, it is lived in this communion of saints, which means both the company of the holy ones, and the sharing in holy things. When we feel low and spiritually run down, we need not lose heart, because we are still one with those who rejoice with unutterable and holy joy in the presence of God, who already have the vision of light and life without ending. That is why it is so natural for Christians to pray to the saints.

How perfect the story is of our Lady at Cana. So gently she reminds her Son: "They have no wine" *(Jn 2:3)*. In the course of our Christian lives, we often run out of things, maybe even the faith that would let us tell God about it ourselves. But she is there, still present at his side, "they have no love, they have no faith, they have no humility . . .".

In the Church we are all living off one another's faith in this way, but especially off the faith of Mary. It was her faith that made our redemption possible. In a very literal sense her faith is the source of the

Church's faith, for without her faith Christ would not have been born. From all eternity God had prepared her to make that act of faith from which all salvation would flow. This is why we call Mary our Mother, and this is also why it is meaningful for us to regard the Church as our Mother. Faith never means simply your faith or my faith. In one of the prayers in the Mass we say, "Look not on our sins, but on the faith of your Church". To invite God to look simply upon our individual faith might be little better than offering him our splendid virtue! It is not our faith, but the faith of the Church that we present before him, and that means the faith of Mary, the faith of all those many people who have made the Body of Christ healthy and glorious; we, when we are weak and poor, can live off their faith. "Jesus, looking upon *their* faith, said to the man, 'Son, your sins are forgiven' " *(Mt 9:2)*.

In a different way all of us live off the faith of Peter, the Rock upon which Christ built his Church. His was a very different kind of faith. He had none of the quiet trust of our Lady. His faith was impetuous and erratic, subject to short-lived enthusiasms and chronic misunderstandings. He was not at all the obvious person to choose to be the first pope! St Paul or St John would seem to be much more suitable, reliable candidates. But our Lord chose St Peter, and his very weakness is our strength. He knew how utterly dependent he must be on Christ, he knew that it was no strength of his own that kept him from going the way of Judas Iscariot. And so he was chosen to be the one to "strengthen his brethren" because he knew what it was to be strengthened himself *(Lk 22:31f)*.

Then there are all our various patrons, patrons of our institutions, patrons of our nations, patrons of our religious Orders, our own personal patrons. Our Lord seems categorical enough when he says, "Call no man father" *(Mt 23:9)*; but St Paul knew full well that he was the father and mother of his converts *(1 Cor 4:15; Gal 4:19)*, and the Church has gratefully experienced down the centuries how some men and women do have a marvellous gift of bringing others to birth in Christ, and nurturing their life with fatherly or motherly devotion. This does not contradict our Lord's words, because, as St Paul makes explicit *(Eph 3:15)*, all fatherhood on earth derives from the Fatherhood of God, and is exercised within his Fatherhood. It is indeed his Fatherhood which is expressed in all human fatherhood.

Dominicans have always loved to turn to St Dominic, who promised that he would be even more help to us after his death than he was before.[81] And traditionally all religious Orders have placed great trust in the prayers of their holy founders and foundresses.

We should not be ashamed to receive God's gifts through one another's ministry. This was the way God wanted it to be, that we might all be drawn closer together in love through the experience of living off one another's faith and strength.

And we get a different kind of help again from

the holy angels. They cannot give us the warm, animal, emotional kind of support that we get from other human beings, but the very simplicity of their spiritual vision can help to alleviate the complexity of our animal life. The purity of their praise can come to our assistance when we are bogged down in the turmoil of our sensuality or our emotions and can find no way through. When we are weighed down by our corruptible flesh, we can be lifted up, like our Lord in Gethsemane, by the spiritual joy of the angels.

What a conspiracy there is to draw us to heaven! Even in our dealings with one another on earth, we know how we can be helped by finding ourselves among people who are simple and loving and generous. It obliges us either to take drastic steps to harden our hearts against their influence, or else to succumb and become more loving, more humble, ourselves. And here we find ourselves surrounded by an immense cloud of those who have been made perfect in Christ, and "myriads of angels"!

Of course we should not think that the attention of the saints and angels is turned primarily towards us. Their most essential activity is their life with God, in bliss and adoration. But being drawn into God and into his life, they cannot help but be drawn into his love. His infinite contentment and satisfaction in himself does not exclude a most tender and delicate concern for all his creatures. Not a single sparrow falls to the ground unnoticed, and every hair of our heads is known to him. The saints who are caught up into the bliss of God must share then in this infinite joy that he has in attending even to the minutest trivialities of his creation. Nothing is beneath his noticing; it is we who are sometimes stand-offish. If God thought anything beneath his attention, then it would simply not exist. Things are only there at all because he considered it eternally worthwhile to create just this primrose, that little wren, that rather scruffy donkey.

We must not seek to exploit God or his saints for purely self-centred purposes; but we must also beware of being more "spiritual" than they are. In spite of the dangers of superstition, it is a very sound instinct that leads people, for instance, to turn to St Anthony when they have lost even the most unimportant things.

As Father Faber says, in connexion with praying always:[82] "See what comes of it! Into what a supernatural state it throws a man! He lives in a different world from other men. Different dwellers are round about him, and are his familiars, God, Jesus, Mary, angels and saints".

We should not be too shy of this glorious company in which we live out our Christian lives; we should not be shy of letting our devotion draw us to make friends with our favourite saints. Each different saint shines with a different and unique radiance, and it is precisely in this way that God attracts our different temperaments and tastes to the infinite source of all radiance which is himself.

We should never think for a moment that this devotion to the saints gets in the way of our relationship with God. The saints have nothing at all of their own to give which they have not received from him, and their essential gift to us is his essential gift to them: himself, his own life and truth and joy. There is no mercy in them apart from the mercy of God, no charity, no forgiveness that is not his. Even if, like Moses, they seem to stand sometimes in the breach to protect us from God, even that is only by his appointing.

God is lavish in all his ways, and it is his delight, being the ultimate source of all goodness, to make his creatures not just recipients of goodness, but also sources to one another of the goodness they have received from him. He delights to see his goodness not just in himself, but reflected in thousands of different ways in all his creatures, so that, seeing him everywhere, we may be all the more amazed and happy at his generosity.

We should not think of this in terms of solemn court etiquette, as if God were prepared to deal with us only through intermediaries. It is nothing like that. There is no question of our *having* to go to God through the saints; it is a joyful freedom that we have. God loves to express his generosity in giving us things to give to one another; if we would enter into the spirit of his giving, as we have said so often, then this is part of it.

In the words of Faber's hymn, "There's a wideness in God's mercy", and wideness characterises all his works. He does not just create one primrose, he creates millions of them, billions of them, yet every one is unique. Lavishness is the very law of his life.

The Father is not just God, he is the source of Godhead, welling up, so to speak, in himself, but pouring itself out in the eternal generation of the Son. And the life so given cannot rest in him, but is poured out again, in union with the Father, in the person of the Holy Spirit. Everything is for giving away, even in the life of the Blessed Trinity. Even the capacity to be the source of life is given away, according to the Latin doctrine of the Holy Spirit which we profess: the Father who is the source of all Godhead has given it to the Son too to be the source of Godhead, in being source with him of the Holy Spirit.

Meanness can never reflect God, and a mean heart will never come close to him. If we want to be with him, we must be prepared to live on the same scale that he enjoys. "You have come to Mount Sion, the city of the living God, the heavenly Jerusalem, with myriads of angels in festal array, and the church of the firstborn, enrolled in heaven, to God the judge of all, and the spirits of the just made perfect, and to Jesus the mediator of the new covenant" (Heb 12:22–24).

At the beginning when God made man, he declared, "It is not good for man to be alone" (Gen 2:18). And man was made in the image and likeness of God. It is not good for man to be alone because aloneness would not fully express the image and likeness of God. God himself is not a God who is alone. We cannot expect to come to God just "alone to the alone", as the pagan mystic expressed it.[83] He glimpsed the ecstasy and intimacy that the human soul can have with God, and this is a true vision. But just as the perfect unity of God is expressed in being three Persons, so the incredible intimacy that we have with God, an intimacy within the very relationship between the Father and the Son in the Holy Spirit, is not exclusive of the wideness of the whole company of heaven.

The life that we receive from God is a life rich with the many vehicles that carry it. Our birth of water and the Holy Spirit brings us into a whole world, a whole society. In reading ancient Christian writers, for instance, we find there our brothers and sisters and friends. In praying we find ourselves at one with all those who are in Christ, regardless of the accident of death; and with some of them too we shall find ourselves united in particular brotherhood and companionship. The communion of saints is not just a crowd, it is a company, a fellowship, a community, with all the diversity of intimacies and relationships that that implies.

We are not alone, as we struggle on in the difficulties and obscurities of life in this world. Even when all earthly company forsakes us, we are not alone. No Christian is ever in the position of standing alone against the world. When Elisha and his servant were surrounded by the Syrian army, in a hopeless position, Elisha assured his servant, "Those who are with us are more than those who are with them". "Then Elisha prayed . . . so the Lord opened the eyes of the young man and he saw, and behold, the mountain was full of horses and chariots of fire" *(2 Kings 6–15ff)*.

In our prayer and in all our Christian life, we should let ourselves be helped and sustained and encouraged by the "ministering angels" who lift up our prayers to God, and by the company of the saints. In such a company we can afford to let our voice be heard, even if it is not the most beautiful and well-trained of voices; here there is help for the poor, replenishment for the empty, radiance for the ugly, health for the broken, joy for the forlorn, praise and thanksgiving in abundance for those who are depressed. And it is all for giving away. "Come, everyone who is thirsty, come to the waters; and he who has no money, come, buy and eat! Come, buy wine and milk without money and without price" *(Isaiah 55:1)*.

Even in this valley of tears, we can already begin to live off the wealth of heaven; we are surrounded and supported by a great cloud of witnesses, and so can undertake to run our course with endurance and without losing heart. And even if we do lose heart, they do not lose heart, even if we are overcome by terror, they are not overcome by terror, even if we are broken by grief they are not broken by grief; and we are one with them in Christ, members of one another.

And when the strife is fierce, the warfare long,
Steals on the ear the distant triumph-song,
And hearts are brave again, and arms are strong.[84]

10 "And then the End"

*And then comes the end, when he hands
over the kingdom to God his Father . . .
and when everything is subject to him, the
Son himself will be subject to him who
made everything subject to him, so that
God may be all in all
(1 Cor 15:24, 28).*

It is exhilarating indeed to think of the glory of the saints and the radiant expansiveness of God's kingdom. But in all this the joy of joys and mystery of mysteries is the infinite fullness of God's own being. St Paul, writing to the Corinthians about the resurrection of the dead, is ineluctably drawn on to the very essence of Christian hope: "that God may be all in all".

In all our reflections on prayer, this has really been the golden thread running through them all. As we saw, the very beginning is the simple acknowledgement in faith that God *is*. It is that attitude which lets us take a holiday from trying to be God unto ourselves, and let him be God, let him declare his own "I am".

At the risk of considerable oversimplification, we

112

may say that all the rest of the Christian life is concerned with the progressive purification of this initial act of faith. This is what all the fearful dark nights described by St John of the Cross are about. We have to be stripped of everything that contaminates the essential recognition that God is God.

This means, for instance, that we must learn to place our trust simply in the fact that God is God; we must be weaned from that kind of trust which rests largely or even partly on the feeling of trust, or on the evidence that supports trust. My faith must not be in my own faith, but simply in the objective reality of God himself.

At first we shall naturally be impressed by the many ways in which God is God *for us*, we shall consider his gifts, his love for us, his unbounded mercy. But we must learn to appreciate God in himself, not just as he is for us. He is a firm foundation *for us* because he is firm for himself: these are not two things but one. If we concentrate too much on his relationship to us, even that will complicate the essential simplicity of it: it is only in being related to himself that he is related to us.

Our vision must be purified so that we come to rejoice more and more in the sheer actuality of God. It is not that he is pleasant or good—the Bible and the mystics both warn us against too naïve an assumption that God is "good" in any sense that we could understand. It is simply that he *is*.

Guerric of Igny in a sermon on the Resurrection[85] harks back to the old man Israel: when he hears that,

after all, his son Joseph is alive, he says, "It is enough:
he is alive" *(Gen 45:28)*. There is a true generosity of
contentment here which is integral to the development and purification of our prayer. We must get
beyond even our most spiritual possessiveness, and
find our joy simply in God being God. It is enough
for us that he *is.*

This may be one of the reasons why mystics of all
religions sometimes seem to talk as if they actually
thought they were the same as God. This is no meta-
physical confusion, but the very practical point that
in their relationship with God there is nothing at all
of themselves that they can hang on to. When our
essential joy is simply that he *is,* then we can nowhere
say, "Now *there* is where *I* fit in." *I* do not fit in, I am
not in the picture at all. There is no self-consciousness
in perfect charity. "I live now not I, but Christ lives
in me" *(Gal 2:20).*

This is why sometimes the saints say that they do
not mind if they are damned, as St Paul says he would
gladly be anathema himself if it would help his
brethren the Jews *(Rom 9:3).* Of course this is
rhetorical language, but it is revealing rhetoric. What
they are telling us so loudly is that they do not care
what happens to themselves. Their joy is in God, and
is as impregnable as he is. Even if they were con-
demned to pass the whole of eternity standing on
their heads at the North Pole, that would not in the
slightest damage the fact that God is God.

They are looking for no other bliss than that.
They are not asking God even to give himself to them.

They are not in the picture. All they ask of God is that he be God, and give himself to God.

This may be why sometimes the saints and mystics have speculated in a rather curious way about "Godhead", almost appearing to imply that there is a "Godhead" behind God to which we should ultimately penetrate.[86] Of course there is no abstract and more perfect quintessential deity *behind* God. But could it not be that they are saying that what is exciting and satisfying about God is precisely his Godhead? It is precisely that God is God that gives everlasting contentment.

The perfection of charity is thus essentially the same shape as the most elementary act of faith. Faith punctures the self-sufficiency of our world, so that there is room for God to be God. Perfect charity is when that puncture has become all-embracing, so that we are nothing but space for God to be God. All that we find in ourselves is God being all in all.

Then God is no longer an object to us, nor we to him. He is subject and object to himself. There is nothing outside his utter self-containment and self-reference.

But God's self-containment is also always a self-emptying. Pseudo-Dionysius[87] says that love is always ecstatic in the strict sense, in that it displaces us from ourselves. Because we love, we are no longer the centre of ourselves. So the Father does not contemplate himself in himself, he finds himself in his Son, who is his Word, his Image, his Expression. And the Son finds himself in the Father, and the Holy Spirit exists only as Gift. And in the same ecstasy God gives himself also to creatures, in a giving revealed most fully in the Incarnation. This giving is truly revelation: it shows us what God is in himself. And by the outpouring of the Holy Spirit, we too are drawn to be displaced from ourselves, so that we might live "no longer for ourselves but for him", and that God may be at the centre of us, "more intimate to us than we are to ourselves".[88]

As we are drawn into this divine game of ecstasy, it is hardly surprising that unlikely phenomena sometimes occur, the phenomena that have come to be regarded as typical of mystical states. It must never for a moment be supposed that these are the essential element in mysticism, but they are entirely normal as a consequence of our mortal humanity finding itself plunged into the ecstatic condition of divine love. No wonder the consciousness may be displaced from the body, as in those trance states that we actually call "ecstasy". No wonder the body itself may sometimes be displaced, as in levitation. No wonder people are filled with emotions and intuitions that they cannot account for and cannot contain.

These things, it must be stressed, however abnormal in themselves, are normal in the context of the transformation of our frail humanity into divine life.[89] What is so striking about their occurrence in the lives of the saints is that they are treated so casually, and this is far more healthy than the fascination for such things shown by occultists and spiritualists and some modern Christians.

What is truly essential is not any of these oddities, but the growth of charity, allowing more and more room in our hearts for God to be God, and finding in that more and more contentment and joy.

And this requires, ultimately, the generosity to let ourselves be entirely dispossessed of ourselves. Peraldus tells us to pray always empty-handed: faith brings us before God humble and poor. But charity goes even further. Meister Eckhart says that we must become so poor that we do not even have God.[90] To "possess" God still suggests a division between us, an element of disengagement which allows me still to be conscious of myself as subject and God as object.

The totally unpossessive nature of final charity is suggested by some of the traditional language used to describe our ultimate relationship with God. It sounds so distant to be told that eternal life consists in *knowing* God and the one he has sent *(Jn 17:3)*, or that our essential bliss is to *contemplate* God. Old Simeon seems easily satisfied, if he is ready to die now that he has *seen* God's salvation *(Lk 2:30)*.

But these images surely express the detachment involved in that generosity which rejoices infinitely in God's own joy. They express one facet of the truth that God *is* our bliss, not just the source of bliss. Our eternal happiness consists in God being God.

This is why, again, our heavenly life can be described in terms of praise. It is a complete misconception when people sometimes tell us that "praise is the highest form of prayer" and infer that we should therefore give priority to shouting "alleluia!" all the time. Heavenly life is a life of praise because it is the sheer exultation that God is God. "We give you thanks for your great glory," as we say in the Mass. This exultation may be expressed in exuberant vocal praise, but it may equally well show itself in utter silence.

After all, God has uttered his one all-perfect Word, so what more is there to say? There is a silence of utter contentment. Just as our first hesitant act of faith may include a sigh of relief, that we no longer have to keep up the struggle, the pretence of being God unto ourselves, so a more mature charity may also find itself completely overwhelmed by the sufficiency of God, leaving it nothing at all to do or say or think. God is the subject and object and content of all experience and all perfection.

In this life we can only glimpse what it means for God to be "all in all", subject and object and content of all experience. In the case of some people, the emphasis seems to be more on God as the all-sufficient object, so that their mental horizon is filled by God, leaving them unfit or even unable to attend to anything else. Some of the saints seem to have been like this, and it is one of the motives that drive men to the eremitical life.

On the other hand, some people are more evidently caught up into sharing in God's subjectivity, so that, in a sense, they become less aware of God; instead their whole vision is transformed, and they see everything from a divine point of view. These are likely to be artists and men of action.

These two are not, in the last analysis, different, however much they are likely to diverge in our experience in this life. What God sees in everything is essentially himself; he is subject and object to himself. This does not mean that he does not see creatures: this is precisely what it is to see creatures. Creatures are reflections in almost infinite diversity of the uniqueness and inexhaustible beauty of God. To be a primrose, to be this primrose, is to be *this* kind of reflection of God. And this is most supremely true of man. It is the perfection of all creatures that God should be all in all. It is our being to reflect God, it is our joy to see him. The root and flower of all that we are and all that we experience is God.

It is presumptuous to attempt to talk of these things, about which even the saints find it so difficult to express themselves; but if we leave out all reference to the goal and culmination of our prayer, then we shall inevitably see things in a wrong perspective, and all kinds of unnecessary imbalance and frustration will result. So, however timidly and unsurely, let us dare, sinners that we are, to lift up our eyes to the mountains, to the heights to which we have been summoned by the call of Christ. And if we could only get the minutest glimpse of the beauty and enchantment that is there, what a fire would spring up in our hearts, urging us to come out of all petty self-preoccupation, to find our joy with "him who feeds among the lilies" *(Cant 2:16)*.

Appendix One

"Shared Prayer"

I have deliberately relegated the discussion of "shared prayer" to an appendix, to avoid the impression either that it is something spectacularly important or that it is something quite different from any other kind of praying.

If we are to take seriously the injunction to pray always, then that is clearly going to cover an immensely wide range of different situations, in each of which we must try to recognise the prayer that is there for us to pray. Sometimes the prayer is given in the circumstances themselves, as when an ambulance races past; sometimes it is given by somebody else, as in the liturgy; sometimes we just find it there in our heart or in our mind.

One of the situations in which we must be able to pray is when we are with other people. Naturally this will normally mean a latent, background kind of prayer, like the Jesus Prayer. But sometimes it may be appropriate to have the prayer out into the open. Maybe we will be with someone who needs prayer, or needs help to pray. Sick people, for instance, sometimes have a prayer that they want to pray, but cannot pray it because of their weakness and confusion; a friend may be able to help them pray their prayer, maybe even praying it for them.

Or again, sometimes we may be talking with someone and suddenly become aware that our Lord is there in the midst, according to his promise. And we need not be embarrassed to acknowledge it. There is a story told of a medieval Dominican priory, in which one of the brothers was dying.[21] The brethren were gathered round in the usual way to pray with him. Suddenly the Prior sensed that the Lord himself had come into the room with great majesty and blessing. So he said: "Brethren, let us fall down and worship; I believe the Lord Jesus Christ is truly present". So they all prostrated themselves and, we are told, many of them "felt a devotion and sweetness beyond all belief or telling."

This, it seems to me, is what is important in "shared prayer". It should be perfectly natural and normal for Christians when they are together to find themselves praying together.

It is also perfectly natural for Christian communities of any kind—families, religious, parishes, discussion groups, and so on—to want to organise devotional exercises to do together. It must be accepted at the outset that such exercises should not compete with the Church's liturgy and should never be made obligatory in the same way and with the same seriousness as the liturgy is. But in their own way they can make a valuable contribution to the life of the community. Such exercises might take many forms, such as saying the Rosary together, reading the Bible together, making a common meditation, perhaps under the guidance of one of the group, or maybe simply praying together in silence. Or they may wish just to pray informally with each other.

Should this be the case, obviously a bare minimum of structure is necessary. There must be an agreed time and place. But this need not mean any more than saying that such and such a room is available for prayer between, say, eight and ten in the evening (or whatever hours are suitable). "Shared prayer" need not be a "session" with a beginning and an end, and there may be good reasons for preferring the more informal procedure of simply indicating a room and letting people come and go as they want to. This would certainly meet St Benedict's objection to prolonged private prayer in common. No one need feel obliged to stay a moment longer than his own prayer lasts.

Where the community in question is not a residential one, it may be more convenient to have a slightly more formal time to begin. But even then, this need not entail any elaborate formalities. There is no occasion to appoint a "leader". Anyone can start the praying; the most natural person will be the one who owns the place, the host. And then all you need to do is to "say the Lord's Prayer and let it happen".

Similarly, if a procedure for stopping the praying is needed at all, it does not have to be anything more complicated than, for example, saying the "Glory be to the Father" together or singing the *Salve Regina*.

During the prayer, the essential thing is that people pray as best they can. They should not be too concerned with what anyone else is doing. "Shared prayer" can be a most misleading term, if it suggests that people should be doing something other than getting on with their own prayers. If everyone is getting on with their own praying, praying aloud as and when they feel they want to, then sometimes there will be a spontaneous convergence of interest, and at other times people will be following different lines. It does not matter either way.

It is a pity if anyone keeps trying to attract attention to himself, or if anyone keeps trying to involve the others, for instance by making them sing hymns or recite litanies, or by constantly reading the Bible to them. It is an essential right of everyone present not to join in anything if they do not want to. The rules that are appropriate to liturgical prayer do not belong here. No individual has the right to impose prayer of any kind on anyone.

No one should feel constrained to listen to everything that is said, either. If your own prayer is more urgent, get on with it. If something catches your ear, then listen to it.

It is useful too for everyone to know how to cope with times when prayer dries up. It is, as we have seen, sheer presumption to assume that one can pray for any length of time just because one chooses to. We should not be afraid of just sitting or kneeling in silence. But if the silence too dries up, then we may need to fall back on the Rosary or the Jesus Prayer or a book or some knitting. And if it becomes unbearable, it is probably time to go away, following St Thomas' principle.

If the group has come together simply to pray freely together, then it must be prepared to find that the different people pray in very different ways. It is more than likely that they will begin to get on each other's nerves. This does not matter in the slightest, provided that they know how to cope with it. It is a marvellous opportunity for practising mutual acceptance and charity. But if the group breaks up, it breaks up; it is not the end of the world.

In fact, too much consciousness of "the prayer group" is probably a bad thing. Apart from all the obvious dangers of élitism and divisive influence, it can easily distract attention from what should be the focal point: God himself. Groups, like individuals, can become too concerned with their own prayer, and not concerned enough with God.

In fact, there is really nothing peculiar to "shared prayer" at all. If people do simply come together to pray—just to pray, not to "do shared prayer"—then they may well find, in fact, that they help each other enormously. In the first place, they may find that their presence together mediates a strong sense of the presence of Christ in their midst. This has its foundation, of course, in his own promise; and the knowledge that everyone there is engaged in prayer together can of itself overcome some of the psychological tensions and barriers that prevent an awareness of the presence of God.

Also our prayer can be tremendously enriched and expanded by the prayers of others. And sometimes people will be drawn together into a real conspiracy of prayer, which can be a very positive service of God and a powerful help to men.

The experience of praying together can draw people together in deep love. It clearly also has great potential for mutual intercession.

But none of this is peculiar to shared prayer. Christians help each other to pray and help each other in prayer in all kinds of ways, and it is not only prayer groups that breed charity. There should be no need for anyone to define himself as either a practitioner or a non-practitioner of shared prayer.

Let us receive with joy the new freedom that we have found to pray with one another. But let us not turn that freedom into a new way of binding ourselves or other people.

On all of this, may I refer the reader to my earlier book, *Did you receive the Spirit?*, which deals more fully with specific questions arising in connexion with praying together. And may I beg of him to take seriously the principle suggested there, that there is a great deal that we can learn from Pentecostalism, but that we shall learn it best by dialogue rather than by imitation. Such dialogue will lead us, then, not simply to become "Pentecostals" (or "charismatics" or whatever other label may be substituted in the future), nor to devote all our energies to promoting a "Pentecostal movement" in the Church, but rather to discover yet again, and in a new way, the fecundity and vitality of our own Catholicism, to discover yet again how "things both new and old" are stored up for us within the single stock, the one deposit of faith entrusted once and for all to the Church. Since I wrote *Did you receive the Spirit?* history has obviously overtaken me in many ways; but I am still confident, obstinately so, maybe, that in due course the enduring fruit of our meeting with Pentecostalism will be seen to have come, not so much from the spectacular successes of the Pentecostal movements in the churches, as from the patient and profound interaction of dialogue. As always, the seed must fall into the ground and die, if it is to bring forth fruit that can endure. If the seed is only superficially sown, the immediate results may be impressive, but the crop will perish for lack of good roots *(cf. Mt 13:5–6).*

Appendix Two

The Gift of Tongues

Since many people are worried or excited about speaking in tongues these days, it seems worth while reprinting here a booklet I wrote for the *Bulletin of Christian Affairs*, published by the Holy Name Press, Australia. It appeared as B.C.A. 39 (Feb 1970), and I am grateful to the editor for permission to reproduce it here.

Until just over a hundred years ago, no one was particularly concerned about the gift of tongues, though it is mentioned in the New Testament as one of the gifts of the Holy Spirit. Exegetes duly commented on the relevant texts. Spiritual writers occasionally mentioned it. However, the Christian world was evidently caught unawares by the sudden reappearance of what was, or at any rate claimed to be, the gift of tongues in London, in the early 1830s. This occurred among the followers of Edward Irving, a popular Presbyterian preacher, whose doctrines had eventually led to his excommunication from the official Presbyterian Church in England.[92]

Since then, and especially since the birth of Pentecostalism in the early days of the twentieth century in the United States, tongues has been sensational matter for journalists and controversialists.

Just why it should have generated so much fury, so much ardour, would perhaps be an interesting study in itself! Some have claimed it as the infallible and indispensable sign of possession of the Holy Spirit. Others have regarded it as an equally infallible sign of lunacy or even diabolical possession. In spite of disclaimers by Pentecostals, tongues is widely taken to be the most typical and essential manifestation of Pentecostalism. The result has been that discussion of tongues almost invariably becomes discussion of Pentecostalism, itself an extremely complex phenomenon.

It is high time that the question of tongues was rescued from the various propaganda battles into which it has been drawn. Recently, indeed, there have appeared a very few articles in scholarly periodicals attempting to find out just what tongues is all about. Here my concern is more simple. It is chiefly to examine the New Testament teaching, to see whether the gift of tongues does have there a place in Christian spirituality, and if so, what place. Inevitably this does not leave quite untouched some of the questions raised by Pentecostalism; but I hope it will help us to see tongues in a truer and wider perspective, a perspective defined by the Gospel itself.

Obviously the first question is: what exactly *is* the gift of tongues as it appears in the New Testament? The chief sources are Acts 2 and 1 Corinthians 14. People have sometimes denied that both passages are really talking about the same thing: in Acts 2 it seems that the apostles are speaking languages needed to communicate with the international crowd of people assembled in Jerusalem, whereas in 1 Corinthians 14 someone speaking in tongues is "not speaking to men, but to God", his words being unintelligible to men.

But if we look more closely at Acts 2, we shall see that there too the apostles are not really speaking to men, except indirectly. They were all "filled with the Holy Spirit, and began to speak in other tongues, as the Spirit gave it to them to speak". And apparently they made such a noise that a crowd gathered, and was amazed to recognise all their different languages; but they were *overhearing* the apostles praying and praising God, "declaring the greatness of God".

So someone speaking in tongues is not, then, normally understood by anyone else, nor even by himself: "When I am praying in tongues, my spirit prays, but my mind remains without fruit"*(1 Cor 14:14)*. Sometimes, as in Acts 2, somebody else may understand what I am saying, but that is an added bonus, and not essential to the gift of tongues as such.

On the other hand, this possibility of being understood shows that speaking in tongues is not, as some people have supposed, merely a matter of yelling and shrieking. Nor is there any reason to suppose that it is, strictly, "ecstatic". St Paul is most insistent on discipline in the public use of the gifts of tongues and prophecy, telling us that "the spirits of prophets are subject to the prophets" *(1 Cor 14:32)*. It is therefore up to them to stop and start, up to them whether they speak loud or soft, singly or all at once.

Sometimes, indeed, people speaking in tongues may give the impression of being drunk, like the apostles in Acts 2, or even a bit mad, as St Paul says in 1 Cor 14:23. The general picture, however, is rather that tongues will normally be a fairly sober and quiet affair, something between a man and his God—"he who speaks in tongues, speaks to God, not men . . . he speaks mysteries by his spirit" *(1 Cor 14:2)*. It is essentially a gift for private prayer, in fact. "The man who speaks in tongues builds himself up" *(1 Cor 14:4)*.

It is not at first sight clear why people should speak in tongues at all; what's the point? we ask, not unnaturally. And it is important to recognise that St Paul, even though he says to the Corinthians (who probably did all speak in tongues) "I want you all to speak in tongues" *(1 Cor 14:5)*, also asks "Do all speak in tongues?" *(12:30)*. Speaking in tongues is only one gift among many others, only one possible contribution to the good of the Church. It is therefore not something that everyone has to do.

On the other hand, there is no reason for simply dismissing tongues. It is a gift that St Paul himself values: "I thank God that I speak in tongues more than all of you" *(1 Cor 14:18)*. It is among the spiritual gifts that St Paul encourages the Corinthians to aspire to, in spite of their evident proneness to abuse such gifts *(14:1)*. Further, in exhorting them to prefer the gift of prophecy, he specifically does not intend the suppression of tongues *(14:39)*.

As we have seen, the gift of tongues appears to be

a gift more for private prayer than for public use, and we must now try to locate its place and significance in our prayer life.

When the disciples asked our Lord to teach them how to pray, he taught them to say " Our Father ". Scholars explain that Jesus was authorising them to use his own personal prayer, a prayer that shocked the Jews of his time—we can sense their horror in Jn 5:18: "the Jews sought to kill him all the more, because he not only broke the sabbath, but also called God his own Father". The early Christians recalled the actual word used by Jesus in his own language, "abba", one of the very few Aramaic words preserved in the Greek-speaking Church. St Paul's commentary is theologically very important, when he tells us that it is the Holy Spirit bearing witness with our own spirit who makes us cry out "Abba, Father" *(Rom 8:15f)*.

It is the Holy Spirit, the Spirit of Jesus, who emboldens us to do something we could not possibly do by ourselves, to pray to God as our own personal Father. We are drawn by God's grace into the very relationship that exists between the Father and the Son; it is without measure that God gives his Spirit to his Son made man for us *(Jn 3:34)*; from his fullness we all receive *(1:16)*.

But we cannot grasp that fullness we are given to share. We have only the "first instalment" of the Spirit *(2 Cor 1:22)*. And so, as St Paul says, "we do not know how to pray as we should" *(Rom 8:26)*. The sheer immensity of God's gift baffles and confuses us. Having been led out of darkness into the light of his Face, we are dazzled and cannot see.

But "the Spirit himself intercedes for us with unutterable groanings". We cannot pray for ourselves, but the Spirit, who pushes us to approach God as Father, himself prays in us in a way which God understands, even if to us it is just inarticulate groanings (8:27).

As the great saints and spiritual writers have all told us, there is a mystery about Christian prayer, such that the one praying will often not understand much of his own prayer. It is part of our faith, part of our humility, to let God himself pray in us, without always insisting on keeping track of it with our minds.

Although this mysterious dimension of Christian prayer is obviously not confined to praying in tongues, it surely helps us to situate the significance of tongues in our prayer life.

Even though different Christians receive different gifts from God in an intensely personal way, nevertheless all of them are intended for the good of the whole Church: "to each one is given the manifestation of the Spirit for the common good" (1 Cor 12:7).

Now, the most basic way in which each one of us contributes to the good of the whole mystical Body of Christ, the Church, is by ourselves being healthy members of that Body. And "he who speaks in tongues builds himself up" (1 Cor 14:4). The chief purpose of tongues is to help us become, through the working of God's grace, the kind of people who really embody the Christian life, the kind of people

whose light shines as unavoidably and naturally as
that of a town on the top of a hill *(Mt 5:14)*. This
is the manifestation of the Spirit.

The particular way in which the gift of tongues
shows forth the Holy Spirit is hinted at in Mk 16:17:
"signs will attend those who believe . . . they will
speak in new tongues". Commentators interpret this
in connexion with the whole theme of the newness of
life that is given to us in Christ,[93] who, in the
Apocalypse, is presented as the one who makes all
things new *(21:5)*. "If anyone is in Christ—new
creation! The old things have passed away, look!
new things are here" *(2 Cor 5:17)*. Christians, re-
born in baptism and made new by the Holy Spirit
(Tit 3:5), are surely quite likely to start singing a
new song *(Apoc 14:3)* and speaking in new tongues.

Perhaps one very special function, then, of the
gift of tongues is to express the newness of the Gospel.
In Christ something has really happened; he makes a
real difference to our lives. By the power of the Holy
Spirit we are actually new people. This is the new
wine which cannot be contained in the old wineskins,
and demands new vehicles for its expression.

And this new wine intoxicates. When St Paul tells
the Ephesians "do not get drunk with wine, but be
filled with the Spirit" (or "be full in spirit": the
translation is not certain), "speaking to one another
with psalms and hymns and spiritual songs, singing
and making music to the Lord in your hearts"
(5:18f), he is not being puritanical! He is pointing
to a kind of intoxication far richer and more fulfilling

than anything that alcohol can produce. The Beloved invites his friends to "be drunk" *(Cant 5:1* exactly translated; many of the versions dilute it*)*. When the divine life comes into a man, as all the mystics have told us, he is liable to behave in funny ways; people will think he is mad or drunk just as the crowd thought the apostles were drunk at Pentecost. Men suddenly confronted with the majesty of God in Christ, like St Peter at the Transfiguration, do not know what they are saying *(Lk 9:33)*.

To accept this newness of life which intoxicates a man with God, we must, our Lord tells us, be prepared to become "like little children" *(Mt 18:3)*. St Paul bids wise men become fools in order to become really wise *(1 Cor 3:18)*. We have to step down from our human, merely human, wisdom and grown-upness. In a sense, we have to start again from the beginning. Perhaps there is a certain fittingness that we, new born into the world of divine life, should be no more able to express ourselves articulately than any other newly born babies.

"Out of the mouths of babes and sucklings, you have appointed praise" *(Ps 8:3)*. God, who chose "the foolish things of the world to confound wise men, and the weak things of the world to confound strong men" *(1 Cor 1:27)*, chose also praise from the lips of babes and sucklings with which "to foil the enemy".

And it was precisely praise that the wondering crowd heard in so many different languages at Pentecost: "we hear them speaking in our own languages the greatness" or "the great deeds of God" *(Acts*

2:11). The new song which God himself puts into
the mouths of his people *(Ps 39:4),* new born by the
gift of his own divine life, is a song of praise. It is a
song which they sing in simplicity and joy, and filled
with wonder and amazement.

Once again, this obviously has much wider appli-
cation than just the gift of tongues; but it does help to
indicate the purpose and meaning of the gift of
tongues, for those who receive it.

We must not mistake our Lord's words about
becoming like little children for an invitation to be
spiritually infantile.

Christian tradition has taken St Paul literally
when he says in Romans 12:1 that we are to present
our *"bodies* as a living sacrifice to God"; often it is
only our bodies that we can present. Nevertheless this
offering of our bodies remains unfulfilled until there
takes place also a "renewing of the mind". As little
children, newly born by God's grace, it is quite right
and fitting that we should offer him our bodies in
vocal prayer that makes no sense to us, praying, as
St Paul says, *(1 Cor 14:14)* with our "spirit" (by
which the apostle means the non-rational part of us;
it is incidentally important not to confuse this with
"praying in the Spirit", which refers to inspiration).

But we must also "pray with the mind" *(1 Cor
14:15)*. "Let anyone who speaks in tongues pray
that he may be able to interpret also" *(14:13)*. St
Paul is not repudiating tongues, in which he himself
rejoices too; only tongues needs to mature into the
companion gift of interpretation, in which the mind

too is transformed and renewed, filled with a kind of intimate knowledge of God which scripture calls "prophecy". "I want you all to speak in tongues, certainly; but I want you to prophesy even more" *(14:5)*.

"Wisdom, coming into holy souls, makes them friends of God and prophets" *(Wis 7:27)*. Our Lord does not want us to be servants, ignorant of the purposes of their master: "I call you friends, because all that I heard from my Father I have made known to you" *(Jn 15:15)*. By the gift of his own Spirit, who searches out the very depths of God, he gives us his own mind: "we have the mind of Christ" *(1 Cor 2:16)*.

Endowed, therefore, with the Holy Spirit, we should "grow in the knowledge of God" *(Col 1:10)*. St Paul prays for the Ephesians that God will give them "a Spirit of wisdom and revelation" so that the eyes of their heart may be opened to spiritual vision, sensitive to God's will, supernaturally enlightened to know him *(Eph 1:17f)*.

It is surely suggestive in this connexion that St Peter explains the outburst of speaking in tongues at Pentecost with reference to Joel 2:28: "I will pour out a share of my Spirit on all flesh and your sons and daughters will prophesy" *(Acts 2:17)*.

The sudden shout of praise that went up in the upper room where the apostles were assembled was already a kind of prophecy; and it was evidently accompanied by a genuine illumination of the mind, so that St Peter, who had so often missed the point of what our Lord was trying to tell him, now grasped the whole mystery of our redemption.

Unfortunately, as 1 Corinthians 14 makes clear, this development does not take place automatically. At least some of the Corinthians seem to have revelled in the gift of tongues, without ever giving a thought to the gift of prophecy or to the renewing of their minds.

The tone of the whole epistle makes it clear that there was a lot of "spiritual" showing-off going on, and it is hardly surprising to find that there was also a lot of intergroup rivalry *(1 Cor 3:3)*, with a lot of immature and unspiritual partisanship, each group celebrating its own favourite apostle and one group even attempting to appropriate the Lord himself *(1:12)*.

The recently published study of American Protestant neo-Pentecostal groups by J. P. Kildahl[94] is a warning to us of just how real the danger is of this kind of spiritual infantilism. He finds that very frequently tongues is used simply as a badge, a sign that one belongs to a supporting and tight-knit group, usually with a strong leader, on whom people can lean and on whom they are generally dependent.

Against this danger, it is important to stress that tongues is not a gift for showing-off, nor should it ever be used simply to identify those who belong to any particular group within the Church. Like all other gifts, it belongs to the whole Church, and one of the major tests of its authenticity is that it helps people to grow up and become better able to be open to the wide world without limitation, to relate to different kinds of people, to accept as brothers those with whom they do not agree.

"Do not quench the Spirit, do not despise prophecies, but test everything" *(1 Thess 5:19ff)*. All "spiritual" experiences and phenomena are in need of being "discerned"—it is on this note that St Paul begins his famous treatment of spiritual gifts in 1 Corinthians 12.

The problem which St Paul has in mind in 1 Corinthians is that of false inspiration. He reminds the Corinthians that even as pagans they were familiar with inspiration. It is important to distinguish between the inspiration that comes from God, and other kinds. And it is important to realise that speaking in tongues is no more exempt from this need for discernment than any other "spiritual" manifestation. People speaking in tongues are not *necessarily* always acting under obedience to the Holy Spirit.

But the more normal hazard is not so much false inspiration. It is rather that "spiritual" manifestations can get divorced from their context in a whole spiritual life. St Paul uses the ambiguity of the word "spiritual" to tease the Corinthians: they are full of spiritual gifts, yet they are not spiritual at all: they are thoroughly carnal, with all their rivalry and élitism *(1 Cor 3:1)*.

Our Lord issues a very stern warning on this subject: "Many will say on that day (the day of judgment) 'Lord, Lord, did we not prophesy in your name and cast out demons in your name and work many miracles in your name?' and then I will tell them, 'I do not know you'" *(Mt 7:22f)*.

It is possible to produce all the outward signs of faith, all the outward evidences of the Holy Spirit, without the reality of faith, without the reality of the Holy Spirit. The Christian life does not consist essentially of signs and "spiritual" manifestations, even though these may be the normal expression, in some circumstances, of the presence of Christ. Tongues and other such gifts are a "manifestation of the Spirit", but they are not themselves the Spirit. The Christian life consists essentially in love, that divine love poured out in our hearts by the Holy Spirit, whose chief exemplar is the love of our Lord himself.

It is possible to "speak in tongues of men and of angels" without having that love. And it is worthless. It is possible "to have prophecy so as to know all mysteries" without having that love. It is nothing.

And so the chief principle of discernment is that one given by our Lord : "By their fruits you will know them" *(Mt 7:16)*. What needs to be examined is not so much the isolated "spiritual" phenomenon, tongues or whatever else it may be, but rather the whole tenor of a man's life. This alone will show whether he is motivated by the Holy Spirit, or simply by the desire to show off, or the competitive need to identify himself with some group he regards as specially spiritual or privileged.

And the fruits that help discernment must not be confused with any other kind of external works; works of charity, devotion to scripture, hours of prayer, all

these things are as ambiguous as any other "manifestation of the Spirit". Where the Holy Spirit is, we shall
expect to find them too; but just because they are
there, it does not follow that the Holy Spirit is there.

Listen to St James' account of how to recognise
"the wisdom that comes from above" *(3:17f)*: it is
"first of all pure, then it is peaceful, yielding, open to
argument, full of mercy and good fruits, impartial,
not showing off; the fruit of righteousness is sown in
peace by those who make peace".

There are, in fact, no external criteria guaranteed
to yield true discernment. Discernment is itself a
working of "spirit" *(1 Cor 12:10)*, and as such it too
needs discerning. It is by the Spirit that we recognise
the Spirit.

And so the very impossibility of ever being *quite*
sure, forces us back to the really fundamental thing in
all true spirituality. This is an utter humility before
God, and whole-hearted confidence in his guiding
hand, his tender care for us, his readiness to forgive
and rescue us from our sins, his everlasting and un-
failing Providence. Growth in such humility and faith
is the surest evidence that it is really the Holy Spirit at
work in us.

Notes

1. *Conl.* IX 36.
2. Rule 20, 4.
3. *Regula Solitariorum* 31 & 32 (PL 103 : 619ff).
4. See Larry Christenson, Four steps to the prayer of faith. (Renewal 30 (Dec. 1970-Jan. 1971) p. 6.)
5. Cf. Hugh of St Victor, *Expos. in Reg. S. Aug.,* 3 (PL 176 : 892). The ascription to Hugh is not certain.
6. Cloud of Unknowing, ch. 37. It is not original: cf. Peraldus, *De Eruditione Religiosorum* VI ch. 7 (in Maxima Bibliotheca Veterum Patrum, Lyon 1677, vol. 25); *de Virtutibus* p. clxxiii v (a) (I quote from the Paris edition of 1519), where it is ascribed to St Bernard.
7. *Ep. ad Probam* (130), 20.
8. Autobiography, III 26.
9. IIa IIae q.83 a. 14.
10. *De Virt.* p. clxxi v (b) (see Note 6).
11. *Mart. Polycarpi,* 7 and 8.
12. *De Virt.* p. clxxi v (b) (see Note 6).
13. Augustine, *Conf.* VI 3, 3.
14. Nine Ways of Prayer (Analecta O.P. xv (1922) pp. 93ff), especially the 6th way.
15. Cf. P. Radó, *Enchiridion Liturgicum* (Herder, 1966), p. 433. The new rubrics of 1960 still included this rule. It was only in 1973 that it was officially declared to apply no longer (Notitiae 82 (1973) p. 150).
16. Inner Life of Dame Gertrude More, ch. 8.
17. Dialogue, ch. 30.
18. IIa IIae q.83 a.12.
19. On Ureisun of ure Louerde, 18ff (in The Wohunge of ure Lauerd, ed. W. Meredith Thompson, E.E.T.S. 241).
20. IIa IIae q.83 a.13.
21. Cassian, *Conl.* IX 31.
22. Athanasius, *Contra Gentes* 4.
23. Apophthegmata Patrum, Arsenius 30 (PG 65 : 97). Eusebius, H.E. II 23, 78; repeated often in the Middle Ages, e.g. Jean de Mailly, Legenda Aurea, etc.

24. A. Hamman, *Prières Eucharistiques* (Foi Vivante, 1969), no. 4.
25. Jean de Mailly, Legenda Aurea, etc.
26. Nine Ways of Prayer (see Note 14), 4th way.
27. Vööbus, History of Asceticism in the Syrian Orient II p. 291.
28. Nine Ways of Prayer (see Note 14), 2nd way.
29. Ibid. Prologue.
30. IIa IIae q.83 a.12.
31. *Acta Canon.* (Bologna) 37 (Monumenta O.P. Historica XVI).
32. *Peregrinatio Aetheriae* 24, 10.
33. Cassian, *Conl.* IX 27.
34. M. Trouncer, Miser of Souls (London, 1959), p. 200.
35. *Acta Canon.* (Toulouse) 18 (see Note 31).
36. *Regula Magistri* 48, 10.
37. Apophthegmata Patrum, Poemen 92 (PG 65:344).
38. Leander Pritchard, Life and Writings of Fr Baker (Catholic Records Society vol. 33) 261.
39. The chief sources are the works of Nicephorus the Solitary; Pseudo-Symeon; Gregory of Sinai (all from the Philokalia), and The Way of a Pilgrim. Detailed references are not given, as the account here is a synthetic one, and, following the example of the first Russian editors of the Philokalia, I have presumed to interpret and adapt the material, in a small way, for use today.
40. Apophthegmata Patrum, Ethiopic Collection 13, 26. French translation in *Les Sentences des Pères du Désert*, Nouveau Receuil (Solesmes, 1970).
41. Frances M. Comper, The Life & Lyrics of Richard Rolle, p. 232.
42. Most accessible now is part of the controversy between Domingo de Soto and Ambrosius Catharinus: Ambrosius Catharinus, *De Certitudine Gratiae*, in *Enarrationes, Assertationes, Disputationes* (reprinted in 1964 by Gregg); Domingo de Soto, *Apologia,* reprinted with his *De Natura et Gratia* (Gregg, 1965).
43. Ian Oswald, Sleep (Pelican paperback), p. 127.
44. *De Spec. Car.* II 56 (quoted from the ET by Geoffrey Webb and Adrian Walker: *The Mirror of Charity,* London, 1962, p. 66).
45. *In Cant.,* Serm. 20.
46. Sennett, The Uses of Disorder (Pelican books), pp. 35ff.
47. A Pistle of Discrecioun of Stirrings (in Deonise Hid Divinite, ed. Phyllis Hodgson, E.E.T.S. 231), p. 68.

48. Cloud of Unknowing, ch. 4.
49. Guigo II, *Scala Claustralium* 8; Bernard, *in Cant.*, Serm. 57.
50. *In Cant.* II 181-2, quoted from the ET by Columba Hart (Cistercian Fathers 6).
51. Meditations III 196-7.
52. Cf. Augustine, *Solil.* II 1.
53. Experiment in Criticism (Cambridge U.P. paperback), p. 94.
54. Cf. Art of Prayer, An Orthodox Anthology, trans. Kadloubovsky & Palmer (Faber 1966), pp. 59; 184, etc.
55. Vatican II, Constitution on the Liturgy, 7; 8; 10.
56. Ibid. 26; 41.
57. Cf. Jordan of Saxony, Letter 51 in the edition by P. A. Walz (Rome 1951).
58. Didache 8, 3; *Institutio Generalis de Liturgia Horarum* 194.
59. Cf. Introit for the Mass of the 2nd Sunday of Eastertide.
60. F. E. Brightman, Liturgies, pp. 24; 62; 341.
61. A. J. Festugière O.P., George Herbert (Paris 1971), pp. 63f.
62. Imitation of Christ, IV 15, 14.
63. IIa IIae q.83 a. 1 ad 1.
64. Ibid. a. 6.
65. *De Virt.* p. clxxiv v (a) (see Note 6).
66. *De Erud. Praedicatorum* in *De Vita Regulari*, II pp. 426-7 (ed. J. J. Berthier). There is an ET edited by Walter M. Conlon O.P., London, 1955.
67. *De Virt.* p. clxviii v (b) (see Note 6).
68. Cf. Henri Ghéon, Saint Vincent Ferrer (London, 1939), p. 181f.
69. St Catherine, Dialogue, ch. 15; Julian of Norwich, ch. 41.
70. Raymond of Capua, Life of St Catherine of Siena, trans. George Lamb (London, 1960), p. 229.
71. *De Spec. Car.* II 73 (ET p. 76, see Note 44).
72. Vatican II, Constitution on the Church, 3.
73. Gregory Thaumaturgus, Panegyric to Origen, xii 149.
74. Cf. Peraldus, *De Virt*, p. clxxxi r (b) (see Note 6).
75. Vie d'Alexandre L'Acémète, 7 (Patrologia Orientalis VI, p. 662); Athanasius, Life of Anthony, 40.
76. *Acta Canon.* (Bologna) 21; *Legenda Petri Ferrandi* 20 (see Note 31).
77. Cf. Malleus Maleficarum I q.3 (ET by Montague Summers, reprinted Arrow paperback, p. 82).
78. Dialogue, ch. 7.
79. Cf. Odes of Solomon 7, 3ff, etc.
80. *Eth. Nic.* VIII 1115a7-9.

81. Jordan, *Libellus* 93 (see Note 31).
82. Growth in Holiness, ch. 15.
83. Plotinus, Enneads VI 9, 11.
84. Hymn by W. W. How, "For all the saints".
85. Sermon 33, 1st sermon for Easter (Cistercian Fathers 32).
86. See James M. Clarke, Meister Eckhart (London 1957), p. 40.
87. *De Div. Nom.* ch. 4 (PG 2:712).
88. Augustine, *Conf.* III 6.
89. Cf. J. G. Arintero, Stages in Prayer (trans. Kathleen Pond, London, 1957), pp. 68; 80ff.
90. Sermon 32 in the edition of Josef Quint;=87 (Pfeiffer). It is believed to be genuine.
91. *Vitae Fratrum* (Monumenta O.P. Historica I), p. 250. ET by P. Conway O.P., The Lives of the Brethren (London 1955), p. 216.
92. Cf. Gordon Strachan, The Pentecostal Theology of Edward Irving (London 1973).
93. Cf. C. E. B. Cranfield, The Gospel According to Saint Mark (C.U.P. 1959), ad loc.
94. John P. Kildahl, The Psychology of Speaking in Tongues (London 1972).

Persons and Sources

AELRED OF RIEVAULX, St. 1109-67. Famous English Cistercian writer; friend of St Bernard. See Aelred of Rievaulx, by Aelred Squire (London 1969).

ALEXANDER AKOIMETES. A wandering monk of the eastern Church. Died c. 430. Although by his time, his kind of monasticism was not in favour with Church authorities, he embodies a very traditional kind of Syrian asceticism, and at least one of his followers was canonised.

AMBROSE, St. c. 339-97. Bishop of Milan, doctor of the Church.

ANSELM, St. c. 1033-1109. Archbishop of Canterbury. His Meditations had a considerable effect on medieval piety.

ANTHONY the GREAT, St. c. 269. He became a solitary in the Egyptian desert; he is regarded as the Father of Monks. The Life by St Athanasius soon became a spiritual classic, and was one factor in the conversion of St Augustine.

APOPHTHEGMATA PATRUM. Collections of sayings and doings of the old monks, the Desert Fathers. They form a marvellous source of monastic "case law". Helen Waddell, The Desert Fathers, gives a selection in English translation (Fontana paperback).

ARINTERO, J. G. Dominican theologian and spiritual director, who taught at Salamanca. 1860-1928. He was one of the pioneers of the revival of mystical theology as a serious part of theology.

ATHANASIUS, St. Bishop of Alexandria, friend of the Egyptian monks. c. 296-373. Doctor of the Church.

AUGUSTINE of HIPPO, St. Bishop of Hippo (in what is now Algeria). 354-430. His autobiographical Confessions became a classic. Doctor of the Church.

BAKER, Father AUGUSTINE. English Benedictine monk and spiritual writer. 1575-1641. His Holy Wisdom enjoyed long popularity.

BARSANUPHIUS, St. Died c. 543. An Egyptian who lived as a recluse in Gaza, communicating with his numerous disciples through an intermediary in letters, many of which survive, and which are masterpieces of spiritual direction.

BENEDICT, St. c.480-c.550. Father of western monasticism. His Rule is the basic document for all western monks.

BERNARD, St. 1090-1153. Abbot of the Cistercian monastery of Clairvaux, he is the best known of all the Cistercian Fathers, and is regarded as the last of the Fathers of the Church. His Sermons on the Song of Songs are a spiritual classic, as is his treatise on the Steps of Humility.

CASSIAN, St JOHN. The interpreter of eastern monasticism to the Latin west, he eventually settled in Marseilles. c. 360-c. 430. He was a friend of Pope Leo I and enjoyed great authority in his own day, and became the standard spiritual reading of western monks, a position he held well into the middle ages. His sanctity, though not widely celebrated, is undoubted and has been officially recognised.

CATHARINUS, AMBROSIUS. c. 1484-1553. A controversial Dominican theologian, who fell out with the scholastic orthodoxy of his day, but was in high standing with the Papal court. He was one of the papal theologians at the Council of Trent. The most detailed and sympathetic account of his work is the article on him by M. M. Gorce in Dictionnaire de Théologie Catholique XII 2418ff.

CATHERINE of SIENA, St. Dominican sister. 1347-1380. She was a great mystic and spiritual teacher, as well as playing a very public part in the affairs of her time. She was declared a doctor ƒ the Church in 1970.

CLEMENT OF ALEXANDRIA. c.150-c.215. One of the first Christian humanists. He was for a long time regarded as a saint.

CLOUD OF UNKNOWING. A well-known anonymous mystical treatise written in English in the fourteenth century.

CURÉ d'ARS (St John Mary Vianney). Unlettered parish priest in France, who became one of the most famous priests in Europe, whose confessional was filled with penitents day and night from far and wide. 1786-1859.

DIDACHE. An ancient book of Christian instructions, possibly dating from the 1st century.

DIONYSIUS (Pseudo—). c. 500. Some eastern Christian produced a corpus of highly obscure but very important mystical, theological writings, which he placed under the name of Dionysius the Areopagite, thus claiming for them almost apostolic authority. They were rapidly taken up as a major authority, especially in the western Church.

DOMINIC, St. Born in the north of Spain in 1170, he became a Canon, and then founded the Order of Preachers in 1215. He died in 1221. He was a man of immense charm, and great breadth of vision and compassion. Contrary to the previous tradition of religious life, he believed in the virtue of laughter. On the occasion of the centenary celebrations in Rome in 1970, Cardinal Villot described him as a man who was "stupefyingly free".

ECKHART, Meister. c. 1260-1327. German Dominican theologian and mystic. He enjoyed great fame as a spiritual director, but his daring language got him into trouble with ecclesiastical authority; the orthodoxy of his intentions is not in doubt, even though he has been claimed by some as a forerunner of all kinds of odd doctrines.

EPHREM, St. The most famous luminary of the Syriac Church. Died 373. He was a monk, a scholar, and one of the great religious poets of the world.

EUSEBIUS. Bishop of Caesarea, and the first Church historian c.260-c.340.

EVAGRIUS PONTICUS. 346-399. One of the greatest masters of the spiritual life and of psychology in ancient monasticism; but his theological and philosophical speculation led him into wild heresy, which incurred condemnation at successive Church councils. His ascetic writings have continued to enjoy great authority. See the excellent edition of his *Practicus* by Antoine and Claire Guillaumont (Sources Chrétiennes 170), with a full introduction; also the ET of the *Practicus* and the treatise on Prayer by J. E. Bamberger (Cistercian Studies 4).

FABER, Father F. W. 1814-1863. One of the leading English converts to Catholicism in the 19th century; founder of the Brompton Oratory. He was a prolific writer, with considerable theological and spiritual good sense. Some of his hymns have become classics.

FRANCIS of ASSISI, St. A favourite among saints. 1182-1226. He was filled with a romantic love of poverty, which he called his "Lady"; he received in his body the marks of our Lord's Passion.

GREGORY the GREAT, St. c. 540-604, Pope from 590. One of the greatest of early Latin spiritual writers and monastic theologians.

GREGORY of SINAI, St. A Greek monastic spiritual writer. Died 1346.

GREGORY THAUMATURGUS, St. c.213-c.270. He studied under Origen, and his Panegyric to Origen gives us a vivid picture of the great master's attractiveness and methods.

GRIMLAC. The author of a rule for solitaries, about whom nothing is known. He lived in the 10th century.

GUERRIC of IGNY. Cistercian writer. He became abbot of Igny in 1138.

GUIGO I, Bl. The great compiler of Carthusian legislation, and author of some remarkable Meditations. He became Prior of the Grande Chartreuse in 1109.

GUIGO II. Died c. 1193. Also a Carthusian. His *Scala Claustralium* was one of the most popular spiritual books in the middle ages, and circulated in various forms, ascribed to various authors. It was translated into English by an unknown spiritual writer of considerable merit himself.

GUILLERAND, Augustin. A modern Carthusian spiritual writer.

HERMAS. 2nd century Roman Christian, author of some very extraordinary and important writings, gathered together under the name of The Shepherd, which at one time was treated as being on a level with canonical scripture. He lets us see something of the everyday Christianity of his time.

HUGH of ST VICTOR. Died 1142. A Canon of St-Victor in Paris, a prolific writer of every kind of book.

HUMBERT of ROMANS, Bl. In 1254 he became the Fifth Master General of the Dominicans.

IGNATIUS of ANTIOCH, St. One of the early Christian martyrs (c. 107), and author of some of the finest early Christian writings, in which his fervent faith and love of God is expressed and his passionate concern for the unity and well-being of the Church.

IGNATIUS of LOYOLA, St. c. 1491-1556. Founder of the Jesuits, and author of the well-known Spiritual Exercises, which became one of the most popular spiritual classics of the western Church, and was even adapted in Greek by Nicodemus of the Holy Mountain.

IRENAEUS of LYONS, St. Bishop of Lyons and the first major post-biblical theologian of the Church. c.130-c.200.

JOHANNAN of EPHESUS. Died 586. Important Syrian church historian, and a leader in the Monophysite Church.

JOHN of ST THOMAS. Spanish Dominican. 1589-1644. He devoted himself to theology, and especially the theology of St Thomas Aquinas.

JOHN of THE CROSS, St. 1542-1591. The mystical doctor of the Church.

JORDAN of SAXONY, Bl. St Dominic's successor as Master General of the Dominicans; his correspondence with Bl. Diana d'Andalò, a Dominican nun and his spiritual daughter, is a treasure of medieval spirituality and a classic instance of spiritual friendship. He died in a shipwreck in 1237. Gerald Vann translated his letters in To Heaven with Diana! (London, 1960).

JULIAN of NORWICH. A lady recluse; one of the most attractive of the English mystics. c. 1342-1413.

LACTANTIUS. c.240-c.320. Christian apologist.

LEGENDA AUREA. The most successful of all medieval collections of lives of the saints, it was compiled by the Dominican James of Voragine, archbishop of Genoa (c. 1230-c. 1298).

MAILLY, JEAN de. Another Dominican compiler of lives of the saints; the first edition of his collection dates from about 1225.

MALLEUS MALEFICARUM. This became the standard textbook on witchcraft in the later middle ages and into the 17th century. It was written in 1486 by two Dominicans. It contains some interesting and important observations, and is not without compassion, even though it was written chiefly for the use of Inquisitors.

MORE, GERTRUDE Dame. Benedictine nun, directed by Augustine Baker.

NICEPHORUS. A Byzantine spiritual writer, of whom little survives and less is known. He wrote one of the most important treatises on the Jesus Prayer.

ORIGEN. A theologian and exegete, who left a deep impression on all subsequent theology, although some of his own teachings were later recognised as false. c.185-c.254.

PERALDUS, WILLIAM. A Dominican preacher and moralist, extremely well-known and popular throughout the later middle ages, but now almost entirely unknown. c. 1200-1271. The best introduction to him is by Antoine Dondaine, in *Archivum Fratrum Praedicatorum* 18 (1948), pp. 162ff. His writings are of considerable interest, as a witness to a pure Latin catholicism, as yet uninfluenced by the new thought of the Universities of his time.

PEREGRINATIO AETHERIAE. A late fourth century account of the pilgrimage of a Spanish lady abbess in the Holy Land and round about. It makes fascinating reading.

PHILOKALIA. An anthology of traditional monastic and ascetic writings, compiled on Mount Athos in the 18th century, and soon translated into Slavonic, and later into Russian. Selections from the Russian are available in English in Kadloubovsky and Palmer: *Prayer of the Heart* (1951); *Early Fathers from the Philokalia* (1954). A complete ET from the Greek is in preparation.

POLYCARP, St. Martyred for the faith c. 155. The account of his martyrdom, by an eyewitness, is of great value and interest.

REGULA MAGISTRI. One of the oldest Latin monastic rules.

ROLLE, RICHARD. c. 1300-1349. One of the more exuberant and enthusiastic of the English mystics.

SEVERUS of ANTIOCH. c. 465-538. Monophysite Patriarch of Antioch, and one of the great theologians of his period.

SOLOMON, ODES OF. An exceptionally beautiful collection of early Christian poetry, from the first or second century. A new edition with ET has recently been published by J. H. Charlesworth (O.U.P. 1973).

SOTO, DOMINGO de. 1494-1560. One of the great Dominican scholastic theologians of Salamanca, who played an important part in many of the great theological controversies of his day. He was one of the theologians who defended the rights of the Indians in the newly discovered lands of America and the West Indies; he also took part in the controversy with the Illuminati. He was one of the Imperial theologians at the Council of Trent.

SYMEON (Pseudo—). Author of an important Byzantine treatise on the Jesus Prayer. It is certainly not by the great mystic Symeon the New Theologian, with whose ideas it is in places incompatible.

THEODORE THE STUDITE, St. 759-826. A great Byzantine monastic reformer.

THOMAS AQUINAS, St. c. 1225-1274. The greatest Dominican theologian, regarded for long as the patron of all catholic theology. Although he was capable of great intellectual abstraction, he was always a great man of prayer. His vision of life is humane and comprehensive. In the "new" language of the schools, he was able to restate the traditional faith, and the traditional understanding of the Christian life.

THOMAS A KEMPIS. c. 1380-1471. Author of the very popular Imitation of Christ.

VINCENT FERRER, St. Spanish Dominican, one of the most famous preachers and wonderworkers of his day. c. 1350-1419. His Treatise on the Spiritual Life, written for Dominican novices, enjoyed a certain popularity; it is available in a rather unwieldy ET (London, 1957).

WAY OF A PILGRIM. A very attractive little book of Russian spirituality, which drew the attention of Christians both east and west to the Jesus Prayer, leading to a great renewal of interest in the so-called "hesychastic" movement of prayer.

WILLIAM of ST THIERRY. c. 1085-1148. A Benedictine monk who became a Cistercian, under the influence of his friend St Bernard. He was one of the more intellectual and reflective Cistercians, but his writings breathe the same spirit of devotion and personal relationship with Christ. His most famous and widely read book is his Golden Epistle, or Letter to the Brethren of Mont-Dieu, which is a résumé of monastic, spiritual doctrine.